In Defense of Anarchism

Robert Paul Wolff

UNIVERSITY OF CALIFORNIA PRESS

Berkeley • Los Angeles • London

University of California Press
Berkeley and Los Angeles, California

University of California Press, Ltd.
London, England

First California Paperback Printing 1998

Library of Congress Cataloging-in-Publication Data

Wolff, Robert Paul.
    In defense of anarchism / Robert Paul Wolff.
        p.   cm.
    Originally published: New York : Harper & Row, 1970, in series:
Harper Torchbooks, TB 1541. With new pref.
    Includes bibliographical references and index.
    ISBN 0-520-21573-7
    1. Authority.   2. Democracy.   3. Anarchism.   4. State, The.
I. Title.
JC571.W86   1998
335'.83—dc21   98-16131
                                                                  CIP

Printed in the United States of America

08   07   06   05
9   8   7   6

The paper used in this publication is both acid-free
and totally chlorine-free (TCF). It meets the minimum
requirements of ANSI/NISO Z39.48-1992 (R 1997)
(*Permanence of Paper*). ∞

Contents

Preface to the 1998 Edition

More than a quarter of a century ago, I published a little book with the provocative title, *In Defense of Anarchism*. The book conformed, I like to think, to Bertrand Russell's prescription for an "ideal form of a work in philosophy" (quoting Arthur Danto in the November 17, 1997 issue of the *Nation*): "It should begin with propositions no one would question and conclude with propositions no one would accept." The premise of the book was quite indisputable: Each of us has an overriding obligation to be morally autonomous; and the conclusion was quite outrageous: A morally legitimate state is a logical impossibility.

The year was 1970, right in the middle of what has come to be called, somewhat inaccurately, "the Sixties," and the book received a great deal of notice for a philosophical essay, virtually all of it negative. Every single reviewer—and there were many—said that the argument of the book was fatally flawed. Jeffrey Reiman even wrote a short book in response, appropriately called *In Defense of Political Philosophy*, in which he undertook to demonstrate the falsity of my thesis. The only person in the philosophical world who agreed with me, to the best of my knowledge, was a young graduate student at Flanders University in Australia, P. D. Jewell, who defended my position in his doctoral dissertation, and then published the results in a book called *By What Authority? Anarchism, the State, and the Individual.*

Nevertheless, everyone, it seemed, read the book, if only to disagree with it. Another doctoral student, Tanya Snegirova, this time in Moscow, made it the focus of *her* dissertation [although, as she told me when she visited me in Northampton, Mass., she had to get special permission from her supervisors to read it]. It was even required reading for a while on the Moral Science Tripos at Cambridge University. I have always been convinced that the real secret of its success lay in the fact that it was a perfect one-week assignment in a course otherwise devoted to mainstream political theory. No professor in his or her right mind would devote a substantial portion of a semester to a work so subversive and unAmerican, not to say undemocratic, but after soldiering through Hobbes, Locke, Rousseau, and Kant on social contract theory, it was rather fun to spend a few throwaway sessions beating up on Wolff.

There were *some* fans, of course. After the book appeared, I received a number of warm, appreciative letters from right-wing libertarians, a fact that gave me greater pause, I must confess, than all of the highly technical counter-arguments in the philosophical journals. But with the application of a certain amount of dialectical logic, I managed to reassure myself that I was really not a closet reactionary.

So the little book has survived, and now, thanks to the gracious generosity of the University of California Press, is to have yet another life. The Press's Paperback Editor, Charlene Woodcock, has invited me to write a new Preface for *In Defense*, suggesting that I might like perhaps to say something about the relationship of this essay to more recent academic work in political philosophy. I will have a go at that, a bit later on in this Preface, but first, since this little book has a rather odd history, I will tell the story of how it came to be.

In Defense of Anarchism actually had its start in 1960 as a reaction to the personal emotional stress I was suffering because of the campaign against nuclear weapons and nuclear deterrence. Then a young Instructor in Philosophy and General Education at Harvard, I had become deeply involved in the rather desperate effort many of us were making to persuade Americans of the insanity of the nuclear arms race. The monstrousness of the dangers of nuclear weapons and the blindness of our elected and unelected leaders drove all of us a little crazy. For me, the breaking point came one afternoon in the Harvard Union, where I began an argument with some Harvard luminary that rapidly descended into a shouting match. I cannot recall now who my opponent was, but it could have been any of a number of people. Harvard then, as now, was full of ambitious, clever, self-satisfied men whose belief in the infallibility of their own intellects led them down the path to success and folly. Henry Kissinger, McGeorge Bundy, Zbigniew Brzezinski, on their way to Washington, mass murder, and the Nobel Peace Prize.

At any rate, the argument in the Union grew more heated, and I must have wigged out, because the next thing I knew, I was running down Massachusetts Avenue toward Harvard Square as fast as I could, in the throes of a full-scale anxiety attack. When I recovered, I decided that I had to back off somehow from the intensity of the daily, frustrating effort to persuade deaf ears that they were leading us to destruction. My way of preserving my sanity—rather a cop-out I thought at the time—was to retreat into political theory, and spend my time thinking about the intellectual foundations of the madness that passed for official U. S. policy. So I spent a good many tranquil hours mastering Game Theory and Collective Choice Theory, as well as the physics of fallout shelters. But I also launched an investigation into the foundations of the legitimacy of the authority of the state.

As a student of the philosophy of Immanuel Kant, I naturally conceived the question of state legitimacy as the problem of making the moral autonomy of the individual—the centerpiece of Kant's ethical theory—compatible with the authority claims that Max Weber had identified as the hallmark of the state. So my first efforts were in the form of an essay entitled "The Fundamental Problem of Political Theory." I read that essay here and there, in Cambridge and then in Chicago, for several years, until in 1964 I was offered a Professorship at Columbia University. By this time, I had grown weary of reading a paper in which I posed a problem only to confess that I could not find a solution, so I had taken to calling the paper, "The Impossibility of a Solution to the Fundamental Problem of Political Philosophy."

When I arrived at Columbia in the Fall of 1964, I was greeted by Arthur Danto, already a member of the Philosophy Department, with a proposition. Arthur had been recruited by Harper & Row to assemble a collective volume of original essays to be called *The Harper Guide to Philosophy*. Harper conceived this as one of a series of handsome volumes, bound in half calf, to be called collectively the Harper Guides—a Harper Guide to Art, a Harper Guide to Music and so forth. As one editor explained to me some years later, when I asked him who on earth would ever read these volumes, Harper was "aiming more at the book buying than the book reading public." At any rate, Arthur had rounded up a stellar assemblage of authors for these essays, but Isaiah Berlin had just turned him down for the Political Philosophy contribution, and he was a bit desperate. Would I write it? Well, I was about to begin a full-scale four-times-a-week psychoanalysis with an Upper East Side analyst at the forbidding price of $25 an hour (my whole annual salary that first year was $11,000) so my only question to Arthur was, "How much is the advance?" Five hundred, he said, and I was in. That was five weeks of analysis.

The next summer, while I was teaching summer school, I sat down to write the essay. Arthur had said something vague [vagueness was Arthur's characteristic mode of discourse] about sketching what was happening at "the forefronts of the field," but I decided to ignore that and simply set forth my own political philosophy. Over the course of several weeks during the summer, I wrote an eighty page essay, entitled "Political Philosophy," which laid out the full-scale version of the argument I had been retailing for five years now on the incompatibility of individual moral autonomy with any state claims to authority whatsoever.

When I wrote the essay in 1965, the Free Speech movement had started at Berkeley, but the Viet Nam War was still in its very earliest stages, and the challenges to authority of any sort, which were to play to large a part in American public life, were still in the future.

The Harper Guide languished, as such things often do. The original editor, Fred Wieck, was replaced for a bit by Al Prettyman, and then by Hugh Van Dusen, the general editor of Harper Torchbooks and still a senior editor at HarperCollins [as it is now called]. By 1970, I had published a number of things in which I had rather optimistically referred to the essay as "forthcoming," but the book market had changed, and it was pretty clear the Harper Guides were never going to appear. Some time in early Spring of that year, I called Hugh Van

Dusen to ask whether I could quote freely from the essay. Somewhat embarrassed, he assured me that I could. Then, a thought struck me. Why not publish my essay as a little independent book? "Great idea," he answered, "we could publish all of the essays as a series of little books. But 'Political Philosophy' is a pretty dull title. Can you think of anything catchier?"

When I was a teenager, I had loved the literary essays of Mark Twain, and at that moment one in particular popped into my head—an attack on the pieties of the literary establishment called "In Defense of Harriet Shelley." "How about *In Defense of Anarchism?*" I suggested. Van Dusen loved it, and so, six months later, only five years after it had been written and ten years after it had been conceived, this little book appeared.[1] The time was right for a book with such a title. It was translated into Swedish, Italian, German, and French, and eventually sold well over a hundred thousand copies in English. Clearly, I had struck a nerve.

The America in which I lived when I wrote *In Defense of Anarchism* was so different from the America in which I now live that those of us old enough to remember the forties and fifties often think that we have somehow mysteriously emigrated to another country. Living as I do in the little town of Pelham, Massachusetts, in what is locally called the Pioneer Valley, I am surrounded by pickup trucks and battered Volvos loaded down with counter-cultural and radical bumper stickers. My

---

1. The complete list of the little books generated out of the manuscript for the ill-fated Harper Guide is rather impressive. In addition to my contribution, there were: *What Philosophy Is*, by Arthur Danto; *Observation and Explanation*, by Norwood Hanson; *The Underlying Reality of Language and its Philosophical Import*, by Jerrold Katz; *Problems of Mind*, by Norman Malcolm; *What is Knowledge* by David Pears; *The Philosophy of Logic*, by Hilary Putnam; *Morality: An Introduction to Ethics*, by Bernard Williams; and *Art and Its Objects*, by Richard Wollheim.

favorite—the one I always secretly take personal credit for—is "Question Authority," which might be a two-word summary of the thesis of *In Defense*. Nothing remotely resembling such a bumper sticker was to be seen in 1965, as I recall.

But it is not only in enclaves like the Pioneer Valley that one sees evidence of the changes. All of American popular culture these days exhibits a distrust of the state and of claims of legitimate authority. When I was young, and movies were Black and White, a character who introduced himself as a member of the FBI could be trusted implicitly. He was the good guy. Now, in movies and on television, the FBI agent is almost inevitably the bad guy. When he shows up in the squad room of a big city police department, he is the intruder, ready to screw up simple justice in the name of some high level, secret, and suspect investigation.

The police too are the heavies. Think, for example, of the marvelously revealing series of Rambo movies. In the opener, *First Blood*, Medal of Honor Viet Nam veteran John Rambo comes walking into a small western town and is immediately rousted by the local sheriff, Brian Denehy. Everything in the movie is designed to make us side with Rambo and view the sheriff as a bigoted, stupid sadist. And yet, the sheriff is of course absolutely correct! He thinks Rambo is trouble, and before the movie is over, several of the sheriff's deputies are dead and the town is on its way to becoming a shambles.

The second movie in the series is even more revealing. Rambo is brought out of prison by the CIA to lead a mission to Viet Nam, supposedly to find POWs still there. But it turns out that the real purpose of the mission is for Rambo to fail, so that the rumor of living POWs is once and for all put to rest. When Rambo, against all the odds, finds and liberates some POWs, the CIA agent actually orders them abandoned. He, not the North Vietnamese who are trying to kill Rambo, is the real enemy in the film.

This theme, that you cannot trust an official representative of the U.S. Government, extends even to implausible comedies. *Manhattan Project* is an amusing film about a phenomenally talented—and, if the truth be told, utterly irresponsible— teenager who builds a functional suitcase-sized nuclear weapon as a project for a science fair. This, we are told, is an unusually powerful bomb, thanks to some hyped up plutonium that looks very much like Prell. When the military show up, ready to kill the lad in order to take from him a weapon capable of destroying a good deal of the surrounding landscape and all the people for quite a radius, *they* are made to look the heavies, and this young kid is figured in the film as just a feckless youth with a sweet girl friend and an overactive imagination.

In the seventies, it was the Left that mistrusted state authority. Today, it is the Hard Right—the citizen militias with their stores of assault rifles and fantasies about U.N. black helicopters. But the utter lack of faith in constituted authority seems to have become one of the staples of popular culture across the political spectrum. The movies I have mentioned, and the countless other bits of entertainment, are popular with mass audiences, which is simply another way of saying that the distrust of authority is endemic. I do not decry this public mood, of course. Quite to the contrary, it strikes me as evidence of the fundamental political health of the American people. Having been tricked, cheated, and lied to for at least the last fifty years, Americans have concluded that they cannot trust their elected officials.

So, if this cry in the wilderness from thirty years ago has become as familiar as an advertising slogan, why a new edition? What does this essay have to say to readers today? The answer,

I hope and believe, is actually a good deal, because although suspicion of constituted authority is currently running high, a real understanding of the foundations of democratic theory and the problematic nature of representative government is in just as scarce supply now as it was when this little book was first written. One way to see this is to revisit the relatively recent flap over President Clinton's nomination of Professor Lani Guinier to be Assistant Attorney General for Civil Rights.

Attorney General Janet Reno nominated Professor Guinier, a member of the University of Pennsylvania law faculty and a long-time friend of the Clintons from Yale Law School days, on April 30, 1993. The troglodytic right, led by attack dog Clint Bolick, immediately initiated a savage campaign to deny Guinier the nomination, and as we have now come to expect, Clinton folded quickly and withdrew her nomination. The focus of the attack was a group of rather arcane law review articles Guinier had written, all on the subject of voting rights and race-based districting.

In what proved to be a pact with the devil, supporters of Southern Black political interests struck a deal with Republican-controlled legislatures to redraw Congressional district lines, gathering together enough African-Americans to create "majority minority" districts. The result was dramatically to increase the number of African-Americans in the House of Representatives—and also to diminish the total number of seats held by Democrats.

Guinier, writing from the left, criticized this tactic, arguing not only that it was politically self-defeating but also, rather more fundamentally, that it simply perpetuated the defects of district-based winner-take-all representation. She argued instead for what she called the principle of "one person one value." By this, she meant some sort of proportional representation that would give minorities of all sorts a measure of representation in the legislature.

Her arguments, as we shall see, were quite strong, and her proposals have considerable merit, but because of a fundamental unclarity about the status of representation in the theory of democracy, she was unable to make her case as strongly as she might have. The intellectual weaknesses of her argument had nothing whatsoever to do with the firestorm created by her nomination, of course. Bolick and his fellow paleocons attacked Guinier because her name was "funny," because her hair was "funny," and also, incidentally, because her theories were supposedly violently undemocratic. Clinton, ever pusillanimous, caved in and Guinier went back to the University of Pennsylvania.

The details of the political fight are unimportant. (Historians will find it hard to believe that Professor Guinier's hairstyle was actually an issue in the choice of an Assistant Attorney General for Civil Rights, or at least I *hope* they will!) But the underlying theoretical issues are extremely important, and as I shall suggest, they are considerably illuminated by the central arguments of this little book.

The core of Guinier's argument is the concept of "wasted votes." A vote can be said to be wasted when it has no impact on the choice of the representatives who make the laws. Now, the American system of representation is district-based and winner-take all. That is to say, Members of Congress represent geographical districts, and the candidate getting the most votes in the district wins the seat. As a result, all the voters who vote for losing candidates can reasonably be said to have wasted their votes, for what they did has no effect on the selection of the person who ostensibly represents them. In addition, all of the votes cast for the winning candidate over and above the bare majority needed to win can be said to have been wasted, though it is of course impossible to say *which* of the winning candidate's extra votes were superfluous.

Guinier quite correctly points out that there are many alternative systems of voting that do not in the same way waste votes. Each of them has certain strengths and also certain weaknesses. Consider, for example, the system used in the first free election in South Africa, in 1994 (this is not Guinier's example). As agreed in lengthy negotiations between the African National Congress and the ruling white-only apartheid government, the new representative body, elected for the first time by all South Africans, was to consist of a lower house, or National Assembly, of four hundred members, and an upper house, or National Council of Provinces, consisting of nine representatives from each of the nine provinces, the representatives to be elected by the Provincial Legislatures and accountable to them.

The upper house was thus to be geographically based, but the National Assembly, which held most of the power, was not. The system worked like this: Each party seeking to contest the election was permitted to nominate a ranked slate of up to four hundred candidates—one for each seat in the Assembly. In the end, no fewer than nineteen parties entered the election. Voters were given one vote, which they could cast for a party slate, not for an individual. When the votes were counted, each party was given a number of seats in the Assembly proportional to its share of the total vote. With four hundred seats, this meant one seat for each quarter of one percent of the vote that the party secured nation-wide. Once the votes were counted, the seats were allocated to party candidates in the order in which the candidates were listed on their party's slates. Thus, since Nelson Mandela topped the ANC's list of candidates, he was the first ANC candidate to be assigned a seat in the Assembly.

In the end, almost twenty million South Africans voted. Seven parties won enough votes to get at least one seat in the Assembly. The ANC, with 62.65% of the total vote, received 252 seats. The Inkatha Freedom Party (headed by Chief Buthelezi) won 43 seats. The old National Party, stronghold of the Afrikaaners, won 82 seats. The smallest number of seats went to the African Christian Democratic Party, which with 0.45% of the vote won two seats.

It is immediately obvious how this system reduces the number of "wasted votes." First of all, supporters of minority parties gain some representation, even if they can only muster less than one percent of the vote nationally. Secondly, there are few superfluous votes. The more voters who choose the ANC, which was the big winner, the larger the ANC's share of the representatives. To be sure, there are *some* wasted votes. Since a party gets one seat for every quarter of one percent of the vote it can muster, a party that gets three-eighths of a percent of the vote will have wasted that last one-eighth percent. But clearly the phenomenon of wasted votes will be marginal, not central as it is in the American system. (The actual results are a bit more complicated than this. Because there were twelve very small parties which failed to win even a single seat, all the successful parties had their vote totals rounded up, except for the Pan-Africanist Congress—Steve Biko's old party— which with exactly 1.25% of the vote was exactly on the mark for five seats.)

There are other alternatives to district-based winner-take-all voting. For example, voters can be given a block of votes which they can either spread around among a number of candidates or concentrate on a single candidate. This permits a minority of voters who coordinate their voting to elect at least one representative. And so on.

The debate in the press over Guinier's proposals, such as it was, proceeded from a universally held assumption that is in fact false. Everyone who attacked Guinier assumed that the current American system of district-based winner-take-all voting is the ideal or perfect form of representative democracy, and that Guinier's proposals were therefore an attempt to address a supposed problem by compromising with that ideal. Thus, it was easy for her detractors to attack her as somehow undermining the foundations of democracy.

But as the argument of this little book demonstrates, all representative government of whatever sort is a compromise with the ideal of autonomous self-rule. The only way to preserve autonomy while achieving collective self-rule is to demand unanimous direct democracy. In other words, autonomy can be preserved in the legislative process only if every person bound by the law participates directly in the making of the law, and furthermore only if each person is bound only by those laws for which he or she has voted. Majority rule of any sort is a compromise with autonomy, and representation, as Rousseau pointed out long ago, is not much better than voluntary self-enslavement.

If this conclusion is accepted, as I argue in this essay that it must be, then we are left with two options: Either we can take the absolutist position that anything other than full autonomy is enslavement—heteronomy in Kant's language—or we can adopt the relativist position that there are degrees of autonomy, and that more autonomy is better than less.

Now if we adopt the relativist position, then the interesting question becomes: Which compromise with the ideal is best? Any form of representation being a falling away from the ideal of autonomy, and all ways of dealing with the inevitability of divided opinion requiring a serious compromise, how shall we arrange things so as to adjust ourselves in the best possible fashion to the imperfections of the world?

Once the question is asked in this way, the debate opens up and becomes a genuine engagement of competing political visions. In the dispute between district-based voting and the South African system, for example, we immediately see that there are many things to be said for and against each arrangement. For example, district-based voting wastes votes by giving all the political power available in a district to the person or party mustering a bare majority of the votes. But the South African system has the distinct drawback that there is no identifiable person who can be said to represent a region, district, or person in the halls of government. Difficult as it now is to command the attention of one's Member of Congress, imagine how much worse things would be if one were forced to make application to the national office of the Democratic or Republican Party! A South African system also requires strict party discipline, which in turn makes impossible the sort of negotiation and reciprocal dealing that in the U. S. Congress does so much of the work of political accommodation.

It could be argued that geographically based voting is preferable in a continental state like the United States in which there are easily identified regional variations in the economic and political interests of the citizens. We are accustomed, for example, to seeing a Democratic and a Republican senator from a farm state unite in supporting a bill favorable to farmers, or all the representatives from a mountain state, Democratic or Republican, joining forces to support a land conservation bill. This sort of regional representation would be difficult, if not impossible, under the South African system.

On the other hand, with a South African system in place, there would have been more than eighty representatives of Perot's party in the Congress after the 1992 election, and that would surely have constituted a more accurate reflection of the wishes of the American electorate.

If we could define a measure of how far a system of representation falls short of the ideal of unanimous direct democracy, then we might be able to rank order the available schemes, and thus demonstrate which is better and which worse. But there is no way of establishing such a measure. Each system benefits some groups of voters and disadvantages others. Which is least undesirable is thus a matter of ideology and group interest, not of political theory. What is more, as the underlying social, economic, and political situation changes, a representational scheme that was least bad from some group's point of view might become extremely undesirable to them. There can be no principles here, only shifting conflicts of interest.

To recognize this truth is both liberating and sobering: liberating because it frees us from the illusion that with sufficient analytical skill, we can somehow hit upon a scheme that will appeal to all rational persons of good will; sobering because it requires each of us honestly to acknowledge the nature of his or her commitments and interests, and not to hide behind false claims of objectivity. The simple fact is that genuine direct unanimous self-legislation is the foundation of the truly legitimate state, and every other political arrangement is a compromise covertly or overtly designed to aid some interests in society and frustrate others.

With this fact clearly before us, perhaps we can now understand a bit better the impulse behind Game Theory and Collective Choice Theory generally, and the work of John Rawls in particular.[2] Growing out of the branch of economic theory called Welfare Economics, Game Theory seeks to predict *a priori* the outcome of situations of competitive interaction in which each of the participants recognizes and takes account of the presence of other agents similarly self-interested. Since it turns out that the sets of cases in which anything like a formal theorem can be proved are extremely narrow in scope, a broader, less rigorous inquiry into situations of collective rationality developed under the titles "Bargaining Theory" and "Collective Choice Theory." All of these investigations have in common the starting assumption that mutual agreement, or unanimity, must be arrived at in order for collective action to be satisfactorily grounded.

When I wrote *In Defense*, these branches of economic theory were relatively new (although John von Neumann had actually proved the fundamental theorem of Game Theory thirty years earlier). Consequently, I treated unanimity as an unattainable ideal, a limiting case designed to highlight the impossibility of a truly legitimate state. Since that time, however, there has been a flood of fascinating work investigating various forms of unanimous decision-making, the most famous and imaginative of which is John Rawls' theory of justice.

As readers will no doubt be aware, Rawls conceived the idea of construing the problem of identifying the fundamental principles of social cooperation as a bargaining game—in effect, a modern version of the traditional social contract. Participants

2. See *A Theory of Justice*, by John Rawls, Harvard University Press, 1971. For an extended analysis and critique of Rawls' work, see my *Understanding Rawls: A Reconstruction and Critique of A Theory of Justice*, Princeton University Press, 1977. Rawls started publishing his theories in the 50s, and there is in fact reference to them in the original text of *In Defense*, but it was only later that Rawls' views gained the enormous currency outside of technical philosophy that they now enjoy.

are, by a process of consultation and negotiation, to achieve a unanimous agreement on the foundational principles that are to govern their social interactions. In short, their deliberations are to conform to the ideal of unanimous direct democracy (although Rawls does allow subsequently for representation and majority rule). Eventually, in response to internal theoretical weaknesses in his argument, Rawls gave up the elements of consultation and negotiation in his theory, and reconstrued the problem as one of pure coordination. Further shifts and changes reduced this game to a problem of individual constrained rational choice. Nevertheless, even in the final version of his theory, we can see Rawls' underlying desire to ground himself in the ideal principles of unanimity and direct unmediated participation in the process of legislation. In the end, I can only be bound by those laws that I have made for myself.

When I wrote *In Defense*, the computer revolution was in its infancy. I myself did not buy my first computer until some seventeen years later—an old clunky Apple II with less memory than my toaster-oven now has and an enormous ugly hard drive with all of six megs on it. When I conjured up the idea of a technologically advanced direct democracy, the most I could imagine was the use of television sets and thumb print detectors. Hence, some readers dubbed this fanciful thought-experiment "television democracy." But now that we have truly entered the computer age, it should be obvious to all that the *technical* obstacles to direct, or plebiscitary, democracy have been solved.

The force and immediacy with which objections to direct democracy surface whenever the subject is mentioned merely demonstrates, if indeed demonstration were needed, that very few political theorists indeed really believe in democracy. Most commentators on public affairs prefer to place their trust in an elite class of professional politicians and policy experts. The fact remains that any legitimacy the commands of the state could possibly possess must derive not from the wisdom of the commands nor from the expertise of those who drafted them but only from the fact that they have been issued collectively by the same group of people who supposedly owe them obedience. Autonomy, which is to say self-legislation, is the only possible ground of legitimate authority.

What then is the message of this little book for the new millennium? In a way, the past three decades have been kind to those of us who question the authority of the state. After Viet Nam, Watergate, the secret war in Nicaragua, and the inanities of Iran-Contra, it is no longer difficult to make the case that the state cannot be trusted. No theorist, even in a drug-induced reverie, could have conjured up a better poster child for anarchism than Oliver North! But is there a positive message to be derived from the critique of the authority claims of the state, or are we left merely with the negative injunction, "Don't trust anyone over or under thirty!"

As is often the case in philosophy, the answer lies in changing the question. So long as I ask, *Under what circumstances can the authority of the state be justified?*, I am doomed to frustration. But suppose, instead, that I ask, *With whom shall I make common cause in the pursuit of our shared goals and aspirations?* This question is eminently answerable, for when I reflect, I find that I have many commitments to others, many shared goals to which I am prepared to commit my energies and resources. But I must never make the mistake of supposing that there is an argument, formal or informal, that will demonstrate that my commitments are the *correct* commitments, that they are the commitments that any rational agent *as such* must make. That way lies precisely the failure that ultimately undermined Kant's ethical theory, and that equally undermines Rawls' modern attempt to revive and revise it. I write as someone who has spent the better part of a lifetime looking for, and not finding, some *a priori* justification for the fundamental principles of morals and politics. I have pursued this will o' the wisp through a series of publications, only to realize that the search itself is ill-conceived. If Political Theory is the search for the fundamental principles of legitimate authority, as I suggested in the opening pages of *In Defense of Anarchism*, then Political Theory is dead. In its place you must put political *action*, guided by reason and directed toward those collective goals to which you and your comrades have committed yourselves. If you have no comrades, then neither this little book nor anything else can help you.

Pelham, Massachusetts
3 February 1998

Preface

This essay on the foundations of the authority of the
state marks a stage in the development of my concern with
problems of political authority and moral autonomy. When
I first became deeply interested in the subject, I was quite
confident that I could find a satisfactory justification for
the traditional democratic doctrine to which I rather unthinkingly gave my allegiance. Indeed, during my first
year as a member of the Columbia University Philosophy
Department, I taught a course on political philosophy in
which I boldly announced that I would formulate and then
solve the fundamental problem of political philosophy. I
had no trouble formulating the problem—roughly speaking, how the moral autonomy of the individual can be
made compatible with the legitimate authority of the state.
I also had no trouble refuting a number of supposed solutions which had been put forward by various theorists of
the democratic state. But midway through the semester, I
was forced to go before my class, crestfallen and very embarrassed, to announce that I had failed to discover the
grand solution.

At first, as I struggled with this dilemma, I clung to the
conviction that a solution lay just around the next con-

ceptual corner. When I read papers on the subject to meetings at various universities, I was forced again and again to represent myself as searching for a theory which I simply could not find. Little by little, I began to shift the emphasis of my exposition. Finally—whether from philosophical reflection, or simply from chagrin—I came to the realization that I was really defending the negative rather than looking for the positive. My failure to find any theoretical justification for the authority of the state had convinced me that there was no justification. In short, I had become a philosophical anarchist.

The first chapter of this essay formulates the problem as I originally posed it to myself more than five years ago. The second chapter explores the classical democratic solution to the problem and exposes the inadequacy of the usual majoritarian model of the democratic state. The third chapter sketches, in a rather impressionistic, Hegelian way, the reasons for my lingering hope that a solution can be found; it concludes with some brief, quite utopian suggestions of ways in which an anarchic society might actually function.

Leaving aside any flaws which may lurk in the arguments actually presented in these pages, this essay suffers from two major inadequacies. On the side of pure theory, I have been forced to *assume* a number of very important propositions about the nature, sources, and limits of moral obligation. To put it bluntly, I have simply taken for granted an entire ethical theory. On the side of practical application, I have said almost nothing about the material, social, or psychological conditions under which anarchism might be a feasible mode of social organization. I am painfully aware of these defects, and it is my hope to publish a full-scale work in the reasonably near future in which a great deal more will be said on both subjects. If I may steal a title from Kant (and thus perhaps wrap myself in the cloak of his legitimacy), this essay might rather grandly be subtitled *Groundwork of the Metaphysics of the State.*

New York City, March, 1970

In Defense of Anarchism

I.
The Conflict Between
Authority and Autonomy

———◆◆◆◆———

1. The Concept of Authority

Politics is the exercise of the power of the state, or the attempt to influence that exercise. Political philosophy is therefore, strictly speaking, the philosophy of the state. If we are to determine the content of political philosophy, and whether indeed it exists, we must begin with the concept of the state.

The state is a group of persons who have and exercise supreme authority within a given territory. Strictly, we should say that a state is a group of persons who have supreme authority within a given territory *or over a certain population*. A nomadic tribe may exhibit the authority structure of a state, so long as its subjects do not fall under the superior authority of a territorial state.[1] The state may

1. For a similar definition of "state," see Max Weber, *Politics as a Vocation*. Weber emphasizes the means—force—by which the will of the state is imposed, but a careful analysis of his definition shows

include all the persons who fall under its authority, as does the democratic state according to its theorists; it may also consist of a single individual to whom all the rest are subject. We may doubt whether the one-person state has ever actually existed, although Louis XIV evidently thought so when he announced, "L'état, c'est moi." The distinctive characteristic of the state is supreme authority, or what political philosophers used to call "sovereignty." Thus one speaks of "popular sovereignty," which is the doctrine that the people are the state, and of course the use of "sovereign" to mean "king" reflects the supposed concentration of supreme authority in a monarchy.

Authority is the right to command, and correlatively, the right to be obeyed. It must be distinguished from power, which is the ability to compel compliance, either through the use or the threat of force. When I turn over my wallet to a thief who is holding me at gunpoint, I do so because the fate with which he threatens me is worse than the loss of money which I am made to suffer. I grant that he has power over me, but I would hardly suppose that he has *authority*, that is, that he has a right to demand my money and that I have an obligation to give it to him. When the government presents me with a bill for taxes, on the other hand, I pay it (normally) even though I do not wish to, and even if I think I can get away with not paying. It is, after all, the duly constituted government, and hence it has a *right* to tax me. It has *authority* over me. Sometimes, of course, I cheat the government, but even so, I acknowledge its authority, for who would speak of "cheating" a thief?

---

that it also bases itself on the notion of authority ("imperative co-ordination").

To *claim* authority is to claim the right to be obeyed. To *have* authority is then—what? It may mean to have that right, or it may mean to have one's claim acknowledged and accepted by those at whom it is directed. The term "authority" is ambiguous, having both a descriptive and a normative sense. Even the descriptive sense refers to norms or obligations, of course, but it does so by *describing* what men believe they ought to do rather than by *asserting* that they ought to do it.

Corresponding to the two senses of authority, there are two concepts of the state. Descriptively, the state may be defined as a group of persons who are *acknowledged* to have supreme authority within a territory—acknowledged, that is, by those over whom the authority is asserted. The study of the forms, characteristics, institutions, and functioning of *de facto* states, as we may call them, is the province of political science. If we take the term in its prescriptive signification, the state is a group of persons who have the *right* to exercise supreme authority within a territory. The discovery, analysis, and demonstration of the forms and principles of legitimate authority—of the right to rule—is called political philosophy.

What is meant by *supreme* authority? Some political philosophers, speaking of authority in the normative sense, have held that the true state has ultimate authority over all matters whatsoever that occur within its venue. Jean-Jacques Rousseau, for example, asserted that the social contract by which a just political community is formed "gives to the body politic absolute command over the members of which it is formed; and it is this power, when directed by the general will, that bears . . . the name of 'sovereignty.' " John Locke, on the other hand, held that the supreme authority of the just state extends only to those matters which it is proper for a state to control. The state is, to be sure, the highest authority, but its right to command is less than absolute. One of the questions which political philosophy must answer is whether there is any limit to the range of affairs over which a just state has authority.

An authoritative command must also be distinguished from a persuasive argument. When I am commanded to do something, I may choose to comply even though I am not being threatened, because I am brought to believe that it is something which I ought to do. If that is the case, then I am not, strictly speaking, obeying a command, but rather acknowledging the force of an argument or the rightness of a prescription. The person who issues the "command" functions merely as the *occasion* for my becoming aware of my duty, and his role might in other instances be filled by an admonishing friend, or even by my own conscience. I might, by an extension of the term, say that the prescription has authority over me, meaning simply that I ought to act in accordance with it. But the person himself has no authority—or, to be more precise, my complying with his command does not constitute an acknowledgment on my part of any such authority. Thus authority resides in persons; they possess it—if indeed they do at all—by virtue of who they are and not by virtue of what they command. My duty to obey is a duty owed to them, not to the moral law or to the beneficiaries of the actions I may be commanded to perform.

There are, of course, many reasons why men actually acknowledge claims of authority. The most common, taking the whole of human history, is simply the prescriptive force of tradition. The fact that something has always been done in a certain way strikes most men as a perfectly adequate reason for doing it that way again. Why should we submit to a king? Because we have always submitted to kings. But why should the oldest son of the king become king in turn? Because oldest sons have always been heirs to the throne. The force of the traditional is engraved so deeply on men's minds that even a study of the violent and haphazard origins of a ruling family will not weaken its authority in the eyes of its subjects.

Some men acquire the aura of authority by virtue of their own extraordinary characteristics, either as great military leaders, as men of saintly character, or as forceful personalities. Such men gather followers and disciples around them who willingly obey without consideration of personal interest or even against its dictates. The followers believe that the leader has a *right to command*, which is to say, *authority*.

Most commonly today, in a world of bureaucratic armies and institutionalized religions, when kings are few in number and the line of prophets has run out, authority is granted to those who occupy official positions. As Weber has pointed out, these positions appear authoritative in the minds of most men because they are defined by certain sorts of bureaucratic regulations having the virtues of publicity, generality, predictability, and so forth. We become conditioned to respond to the visible signs of officiality, such as printed forms and badges. Sometimes we may have clearly in mind the justification for a legalistic claim to authority, as when we comply with a command because its author is an *elected* official. More often the mere sight of a uniform is enough to make us feel that the man inside it has a right to be obeyed.

That men accede to claims of supreme authority is plain. That men *ought* to accede to claims of supreme authority is not so obvious. Our first question must therefore be, Under what conditions and for what reasons does one man have supreme authority over another? The same question can be restated, Under what conditions can a state (understood normatively) exist?

Kant has given us a convenient title for this sort of investigation. He called it a "deduction," meaning by the term not a proof of one proposition from another, but a demonstration of the legitimacy of a concept. When a concept is empirical, its deduction is accomplished merely by pointing to instances of its objects. For example, the deduction of the concept of a horse consists in exhibiting a horse. Since there are horses, it must be legitimate to employ the concept. Similarly, a deduction of the descriptive concept of a state consists simply in pointing to the innumerable examples of human communities in which some men claim supreme authority over the rest and are obeyed. But when the concept in question is nonempirical, its deduction must proceed in a different manner. All normative concepts are nonempirical, for they refer to what ought to be rather than to what is. Hence, we cannot justify the use of the concept of (normative) supreme authority by presenting instances.[2] We must demonstrate by an *a priori* argument that there can be forms of human community in which some men have a moral right to rule. In short, the fundamental task of political philosophy is to provide a *deduction of the concept of the state.*

2. For each time we offered an example of legitimate authority, we would have to attach to it a nonempirical argument proving the legitimacy.

To complete this deduction, it is not enough to show that there are circumstances in which men have an obligation to do what the *de facto* authorities command. Even under the most unjust of governments there are frequently good reasons for obedience rather than defiance. It may be that the government has commanded its subjects to do what in fact they already have an independent obligation to do; or it may be that the evil consequences of defiance far outweigh the indignity of submission. A government's commands may promise beneficent effects, either intentionally or not. For these reasons, and for reasons of prudence as well, a man may be right to comply with the commands of the government under whose *de facto* authority he finds himself. But none of this settles the question of legitimate authority. That is a matter of the *right* to command, and of the correlative obligation *to obey the person who issues the command.*

The point of the last paragraph cannot be too strongly stressed. Obedience is not a matter of doing what someone tells you to do. It is a matter of doing what he tells you to do *because he tells you to do it.* Legitimate, or *de jure,* authority thus concerns the grounds and sources of moral obligation.

Since it is indisputable that there are men who believe that others have authority over them, it might be thought that we could use that fact to prove that somewhere, at some time or other, there must have been men who really did possess legitimate authority. We might think, that is to say, that although some claims to authority might be wrong, it could not be that *all* such claims were wrong, since then we never would have had the concept of legitimate authority at all. By a similar argument, some philosophers have tried to show that not all our experiences are dreams, or more generally that in experience not everything is mere apearance rather than reality. The point is that terms like "dream" and "appearance" are defined by contrast with "waking experience" or "reality." Hence we could only have developed a use for them by being presented with situations in which some experiences were dreams and others not, or some things mere appearance and others reality.

Whatever the force of that argument in general, it cannot be applied to the case of *de facto* versus *de jure* authority, for the key component of both concepts, namely "right," is imported into the discussion from the realm of moral philosophy generally. Insofar as we concern ourselves with the possibility of a just state, we *assume* that moral discourse is meaningful and that adequate deductions have been given of concepts like "right," "duty," and "obligation."[3]

What can be inferred from the existence of *de facto* states is that men *believe* in the existence of legitimate authority, for of course a *de facto* state is simply a state whose subjects believe it to be legitimate (i.e., really to have the authority which it claims for itself). They may be wrong. Indeed, *all* beliefs in authority may be wrong—there may be not a single state in the history of mankind which has now or ever has had a right to be obeyed. It might even be impossible for such a state to exist; that is the question we must try to settle. But so long as men believe in the au-

3. Thus, political philosophy is a dependent or derivative discipline, just as the philosophy of science is dependent upon the general theory of knowledge and on the branches of metaphysics which concern themselves with the reality and nature of the physical world.

thority of states, we can conclude that they possess the concept of *de jure* authority.[4]

The normative concept of the state as the human community which possesses rightful authority within a territory thus defines the subject matter of political philosophy proper. However, even if it should prove impossible to present a deduction of the concept—if, that is, there can be no *de jure* state—still a large number of moral questions can be raised concerning the individual's relationship with *de facto* states. We may ask, for example, whether there are any moral principles which ought to guide the state in its lawmaking, such as the principle of utilitarianism, and under what conditions it is right for the individual to obey the laws. We may explore the social ideals of equality and achievement, or the principles of punishment, or the justifications for war. All such investigations are essentially applications of general moral principles to the particular phenomena of (*de facto*) politics. Hence, it would be appropriate to reclaim a word which has fallen on bad days, and call that branch of the study of politics *casuistical politics*. Since there are men who acknowledge claims to authority, there are *de facto* states. Assuming that moral discourse in general is legitimate, there must be moral questions which arise in regard to such states. Hence, casuistical politics as a branch of ethics does exist. It re-

4. This point is so simple that it may seem unworthy of such emphasis. Nevertheless, a number of political philosophers, including Hobbes and John Austin, have supposed that *the concept* as well as the principles of authority could be derived from the concepts of power or utility. For example, Austin defines a command as a signification of desire, uttered by someone who will visit evil on those who do not comply with it (*The Providence of Jurisprudence Determined*, Lecture I).

mains to be decided whether political philosophy proper exists.

2. The Concept of Autonomy

The fundamental assumption of moral philosophy is that men are responsible for their actions. From this assumption it follows necessarily, as Kant pointed out, that men are metaphysically free, which is to say that in some sense they are capable of choosing how they shall act. Being able to choose how he acts makes a man responsible, but merely choosing is not in itself enough to constitute *taking* responsibility for one's actions. Taking responsibility involves attempting to determine what one ought to do, and that, as philosophers since Aristotle have recognized, lays upon one the additional burdens of gaining knowledge, reflecting on motives, predicting outcomes, criticizing principles, and so forth.

The obligation to take responsibility for one's actions does not derive from man's freedom of will alone, for more is required in taking responsibility than freedom of choice. Only because man has the capacity to reason about his choices can he be said to stand under a continuing obligation to take responsibility for them. It is quite appropriate that moral philosophers should group together children and madmen as beings not fully responsible for their actions, for as madmen are thought to lack freedom of choice, so children do not yet possess the power of reason in a developed form. It is even just that we should assign a greater degree of responsibility to children, for madmen, by virtue of their lack of free will, are completely without responsibility, while children, insofar as they possess reason in a partially developed form, can be held responsible (i.e., can be required to take responsibility) to a corresponding degree.

Every man who possesses both free will and reason has an obligation to take responsibility for his actions, even though he may not be actively engaged in a continuing process of reflection, investigation, and deliberation about how he ought to act. A man will sometimes announce his willingness to take responsibility for the consequences of his actions, even though he has not deliberated about them, or does not intend to do so in the future. Such a declaration is, of course, an advance over the refusal to take responsibility; it at least acknowledges the existence of the obligation. But it does not relieve the man of the duty to engage in the reflective process which he has thus far shunned. It goes without saying that a man may take responsibility for his actions and yet act wrongly. When we describe someone as a responsible individual, we do not imply that he always does what is right, but only that he does not neglect the duty of attempting to ascertain what is right.

The responsible man is not capricious or anarchic, for he does acknowledge himself bound by moral constraints. But he insists that he alone is the judge of those constraints. He may listen to the advice of others, but he makes it his own by determining for himself whether it is good advice. He may learn from others about his moral obligations, but only in the sense that a mathematician learns from other mathematicians—namely by hearing from them arguments whose validity he recognizes even though he did not think of them himself. He does not learn in the sense that one learns from an explorer, by accepting as true his accounts of things one cannot see for oneself.

Since the responsible man arrives at moral decisions

which he expresses to himself in the form of impera-
tives, we may say that he gives laws to himself, or is self-
legislating. In short, he is *autonomous*. As Kant argued,
moral autonomy is a combination of freedom and responsibility; it is a submission to laws which one has made for
oneself. The autonomous man, insofar as he is autonomous,
is not subject to the will of another. He may do what another tells him, but not *because* he has been told to do it.
He is therefore, in the political sense of the word, *free*.

Since man's responsibility for his actions is a conse-
quence of his capacity for choice, he cannot give it up or
put it aside. He can refuse to acknowledge it, however,
either deliberately or by simply failing to recognize his
moral condition. All men refuse to take responsibility for
their actions at some time or other during their lives, and
some men so consistently shirk their duty that they present
more the appearance of overgrown children than of adults.
Inasmuch as moral autonomy is simply the condition of
taking full responsibility for one's actions, it follows that
men can forfeit their autonomy at will. That is to say, a
man can decide to obey the commands of another without
making any attempt to determine for himself whether
what is commanded is good or wise.

This is an important point, and it should not be confused with the false assertion that a man can give up responsibility for his actions. Evan after he has subjected
himself to the will of another, an individual remains responsible for what he does. But by refusing to engage in
moral deliberation, by accepting as final the commands of
the others, he forfeits his autonomy. Rousseau is therefore
right when he says that a man cannot become a slave even
through his own choice, if he means that even slaves are

morally responsible for their acts. But he is wrong if he means that men cannot place themselves voluntarily in a position of servitude and mindless obedience.

There are many forms and degrees of forfeiture of autonomy. A man can give up his independence of judgment with regard to a single question, or in respect of a single type of question. For example, when I place myself in the hands of my doctor, I commit myself to whatever course of treatment he prescribes, but only in regard to my health. I do not make him my legal counselor as well. A man may forfeit autonomy on some or all questions for a specific period of time, or during his entire life. He may submit himself to all commands, whatever they may be, save for some specified acts (such as killing) which he refuses to perform. From the example of the doctor, it is obvious that there are at least some situations in which it is reasonable to give up one's autonomy. Indeed, we may wonder whether, in a complex world of technical expertise, it is ever reasonable *not* to do so!

Since the concept of taking and forfeiting responsibility is central to the discussion which follows, it is worth devoting a bit more space to clarifying it. Taking responsibility for one's actions means making the final decisions about what one should do. For the autonomous man, there is no such thing, strictly speaking, as a *command.* If someone in my environment is issuing what are intended as commands, and if he or others expect those commands to be obeyed, that fact will be taken account of in my deliberations. I may decide that I ought to do what that person is commanding me to do, and it may even be that his issuing the command is the factor in the situation which makes it desirable for me to do so. For example, if I am on a sinking ship and the captain is giving orders for manning the life-boats, and if everyone else is obeying the captain *because he is the captain,* I may decide that under the circumstances I had better do what he says, since the confusion caused by disobeying him would be generally harmful. But insofar as I make such a decision, I am not *obeying his command;* that is, I am not acknowledging him as having authority over me. I would make the same decision, for exactly the same reasons, if one of the passengers had started to issue "orders" and had, in the confusion, come to be obeyed.

In politics, as in life generally, men frequently forfeit their autonomy. There are a number of causes for this fact, and also a number of arguments which have been offered to justify it. Most men, as we have already noted, feel so strongly the force of tradition or bureaucracy that they accept unthinkingly the claims to authority which are made by their nominal rulers. It is the rare individual in the history of the race who rises even to the level of questioning the right of his masters to command and the duty of himself and his fellows to obey. Once the dangerous question has been started, however, a variety of arguments can be brought forward to demonstrate the authority of the rulers. Among the most ancient is Plato's assertion that men should submit to the authority of those with superior knowledge, wisdom, or insight. A sophisticated modern version has it that the educated portion of a democratic population is more likely to be politically active, and that it is just as well for the ill-informed segment of the electorate to remain passive, since its entrance into the political arena only supports the efforts of demagogues and extremists. A number of American political scientists have gone so far as to claim that the apathy of the American masses is a cause of stability and hence a good thing.

The moral condition demands that we acknowledge responsibility and achieve autonomy wherever and whenever possible. Sometimes this involves moral deliberation and reflection; at other times, the gathering of special, even technical, information. The contemporary American citizen, for example, has an obligation to master enough modern science to enable him to follow debates about nuclear policy and come to an independent conclusion.[5] There are great, perhaps insurmountable, obstacles to the achievement of a complete and rational autonomy in the modern world. Nevertheless, so long as we recognize our responsibility for our actions, and acknowledge the power of reason within us, we must acknowledge as well the continuing obligation to make ourselves the authors of such commands as we may obey. The paradox of man's condition in the modern world is that the more fully he recognizes his right and duty to be his own master, the more completely he becomes the passive object of a technology and bureaucracy whose complexities he cannot hope to understand. It is only several hundred years since a reasonably well-educated man could claim to understand the major issues of government as well as his king or parliament. Ironically, the high school graduate of today, who

5. This is not quite so difficult as it sounds, since policy very rarely turns on disputes over technical or theoretical details. Still, the citizen who, for example, does not understand the nature of atomic radiation cannot even pretend to have an opinion on the feasibility of bomb shelters; and since the momentous choice between first-strike and second-strike nuclear strategies depends on the possibility of a successful shelter system, the uninformed citizen will be as completely at the mercy of his "representatives" as the lowliest slave.

cannot master the issues of foreign and domestic policy on which he is asked to vote, could quite easily have grasped the problems of eighteenth-century statecraft.

3. The Conflict Between Authority and Autonomy

The defining mark of the state is authority, the right to rule. The primary obligation of man is autonomy, the refusal to be ruled. It would seem, then, that there can be no resolution of the conflict between the autonomy of the individual and the putative authority of the state. Insofar as a man fulfills his obligation to make himself the author of his decisions, he will resist the state's claim to have authority over him. That is to say, he will deny that he has a duty to obey the laws of the state *simply because they are the laws.* In that sense, it would seem that anarchism is the only political doctrine consistent with the virtue of autonomy.

Now, of course, an anarchist may grant the necessity of *complying* with the law under certain circumstances or for the time being. He may even doubt that there is any real prospect of eliminating the state as a human institution. But he will never view the commands of the state as *legitimate,* as having a binding moral force. In a sense, we might characterize the anarchist as a man without a country, for despite the ties which bind him to the land of his childhood, he stands in precisely the same moral relationship to "his" government as he does to the government of any other country in which he might happen to be staying for a time. When I take a vacation in Great Britain, I obey its laws, both because of prudential self-interest and because of the obvious moral considerations concerning the value of order, the general good consequences of preserving a system of property, and so forth. On my return to the United States, I have a sense of reentering *my* country, and if I think about the matter at all, I imagine myself to stand in a different and more intimate relation to American laws. They have been promulgated by *my* government, and I therefore have a special obligation to obey them. But the anarchist tells me that my feeling is purely sentimental and has no objective moral basis. All authority is equally illegitimate, although of course not therefore equally worthy or unworthy of support, and my obedience to American laws, if I am to be morally autonomous, must proceed from the same considerations which determine me abroad.

The dilemma which we have posed can be succinctly expressed in terms of the concept of a *de jure* state. If all men have a continuing obligation to achieve the highest degree of autonomy possible, then there would appear to be no state whose subjects have a moral obligation to obey its commands. Hence, the concept of a *de jure* legitimate state would appear to be vacuous, and philosophical anarchism would seem to be the only reasonable political belief for an enlightened man.

II.

The Solution of Classical Democracy

———————◆—◖◗—◆———————

1. Democracy Is the Only Feasible Solution

It is not necessary to argue at length the merits of all the various types of state which, since Plato, have been the standard fare of political philosophies. John Locke may have found it worthwhile to devote an entire treatise to Sir Robert Filmer's defense of the hereditary rights of kings, but today the belief in all forms of traditional authority is as weak as the arguments which can be given for it. There is only one form of political community which offers any hope of resolving the conflict between authority and autonomy, and that is democracy.

The argument runs thus: men cannot be free so long as they are subject to the will of others, whether one man (a monarch) or several (aristocrats). But if men rule themselves, if they are both law-givers and law-obeyers, then they can combine the benefits of government with the blessings of freedom. Rule *for* the people is merely benevolent slavery, but rule *by* the people is true freedom. Insofar as a man participates in the affairs of state, he is ruler as well as ruled. His obligation to submit to the laws stems not from the divine right of the monarch, nor from the hereditary authority of a noble class, but from the fact that he himself is the source of the laws which govern him. Therein lies the peculiar merit and moral claim of a democratic state.

Democracy attempts a natural extension of the duty of autonomy to the realm of collective action. Just as the truly responsible man gives laws to himself, and thereby binds himself to what he conceives to be right, so a society of responsible men can collectively bind themselves to laws collectively made, and thereby bind themselves to what they have together judged to be right. The government of a democratic state is then, strictly speaking, no more than a servant of the people as a whole, charged with the execution of laws which have been commonly agreed upon. In the words of Rousseau, "every person, while uniting himself with all, ... obey[s] only himself and remain[s] as free as before" (*Social Contract*, Bk. I, Ch. 6).

Let us explore this proposal more closely. We shall begin with the simplest form of democratic state, which may be labeled *unanimous direct democracy*.

2. Unanimous Direct Democracy

There is, in theory, a solution to the problem which has been posed, and this fact is in itself quite important. However, the solution requires the imposition of impossibly restrictive conditions which make it applicable only to a rather bizarre variety of actual situations. The solution is a direct democracy—that is, a political community in which every person votes on every issue—governed by a rule of unanimity. Under unanimous direct democracy, every member of the society wills freely every law which is actually passed. Hence, he is only confronted as a citizen with laws to which he has consented. Since a man who is constrained only by the dictates of his own will is autonomous, it follows that under the directions of unanimous direct democracy, men can harmonize the duty of autonomy with the commands of authority.

It might be argued that even this limiting case is not genuine, since each man is obeying himself, and hence is not submitting to a legitimate authority. However, the case is really different from the prepolitical (or extrapolitical) case of self-determination, for the authority to which each citizen submits is not that of himself simply, but that of the entire community taken collectively. The laws are issued in the name of the sovereign, which is to say the total population of the community. The power which enforces the law (should there be any citizen who, having voted for a law, now resists its application to himself) is the power of all, gathered together into the police power of the state. By this means, the moral conflict between duty and interest which arises from time to time within each man is externalized, and the voice of duty now speaks with the authority of law. Each man, in a manner of speaking, encounters his better self in the form of the state, for its dictates are simply the laws which he has, after due deliberation, willed to be enacted.

Unanimous direct democracy is feasible only so long as

there is substantial agreement among *all* the members of a community on the matters of major importance. Since by the rule of unanimity a single negative vote defeats any motion, the slightest disagreement over significant questions will bring the operations of the society to a halt. It will cease to function as a political community and fall into a condition of anarchy (or at least into a condition of nonlegitimacy; a *de facto* government may of course emerge and take control). However, it should not be thought that unanimous direct democracy requires for its existence a perfect harmony of the interests or desires of the citizens. It is perfectly consistent with such a system that there be sharp, even violent, oppositions within the community, perhaps of an economic kind. The only necessity is that when the citizens come together to deliberate on the means for resolving such conflicts, they agree unanimously on the laws to be adopted.[6]

For example, a community may agree unanimously on some principles of compulsory arbitration by which economic conflicts are to be settled. An individual who has voted for these principles may then find himself personally disadvantaged by their application in a particular case. Thinking the principles fair, and knowing that he voted for them, he will (hopefully) acknowledge his moral obligation to accept their operation even though he would

6. In recent years, a number of political philosophers have explored the possibilities of decision by unanimity, and it turns out that much more can be achieved than one would expect. For example, John Rawls, in an influential and widely read essay, "Justice as Fairness," uses certain models taken from bargaining theory to analyze the conditions under which rational men with conflicting interests might arrive at unanimous agreement on the procedural principles for resolving their disputes. See Rawls in *Philosophy, Politics, and Society*, 2nd series, eds. P. Laslett and W. Runciman.

The Solution of Classical Democracy

dearly like not to be subject to them. He will recognize
the principles as his own, just as any of us who has committed himself to a moral principle will, uncomfortably to
be sure, recognize its binding force upon him even when it
is inconvenient. More precisely, this individual will have
a moral obligation to obey the commands of the mediation
board or arbitration council, *whatever it decides*, because
the principles which guide it issue from his own will. Thus
the board will have authority over him (i.e., a right to be
obeyed) while he retains his moral autonomy.

Under what circumstances might a unanimous direct
democracy actually function for a reasonable period of
time without simply coming to a series of negative decisions? The answer, I think, is that there are two sorts of
practical unanimous direct democracies. First, a community of persons inspired by some all-absorbing religious
or secular ideal might find itself so completely in agreement on the goals of the community and the means for
achieving them that decisions could be taken on all major
questions by a method of consensus. Utopian communities
in the nineteenth century and some of the Israeli kib-
butzim in the twentieth are plausible instances of such a
functioning unanimity. Eventually, the consensus dissolves
and factions appear, but in some cases the unanimity has
been preserved for a period of many years.

Second, a community of rationally self-interested individuals may discover that it can only reap the fruits of cooperation by maintaining unanimity. So long as each member
of the community remains convinced that the benefits
to him from cooperation—even under the conditions of
compromise imposed by the need for unanimity—outweigh
the benefits of severing his connection with the rest, the

community will continue to function. For example, a classical laissez-faire economy ruled by the laws of the marketplace is supposedly endorsed by all the participants because each one recognizes *both* that he is better off in the system than out *and* that any relaxation of the ban against arrangements in restraint of trade would in the end do him more harm than good. So long as every businessman believes these two propositions, there will be unanimity on the laws of the system despite the cutthroat competition.[7]

As soon as disagreement arises on important questions, unanimity is destroyed and the state must either cease to be *de jure* or else discover some means for settling disputed issues which does not deprive any member of his autonomy. Furthermore, when the society grows too large for convenience in calling regular assemblies, some way must be found to conduct the business of the state without condemning most of the citizens to the status of voiceless subjects. The traditional solutions in democratic theory to these familiar problems are of course majority rule and representation. Our next task, therefore, is to discover whether representative majoritarian democracy preserves the autonomy which men achieve under a unanimous direct democracy.

Since unanimous democracy can exist only under such limited conditions, it might be thought that there is very little point in discussing it at all. For two reasons, however,

7. Strictly speaking, this second example of a viable unanimous community is imperfect, since there is a significant difference between committing oneself to a moral principle and calculating one's enlightened self-interest. For an illuminating discussion of the moral importance of committing oneself to a principle, see Rawls, *op. cit.*

unanimous direct democracy has great theoretical importance. First, it *is* a genuine solution to the problem of autonomy and authority, and as we shall see, this makes it rather unusual. More important still, unanimous direct democracy is the (frequently unexpressed) ideal which underlies a great deal of classical democratic theory. The devices of majoritarianism and representation are introduced in order to overcome obstacles which stand in the way of unanimity and direct democracy. Unanimity is clearly thought to be the method of making decisions which is most obviously legitimate; other forms are presented as compromises with this ideal, and the arguments in favor of them seek to show that the authority of a unanimous democracy is not fatally weakened by the necessity of using representation or majority rule. One evidence of the theoretical primacy of unanimous direct democracy is the fact that in all social contract theories, the original collective adoption of the social contract is always a unanimous decision made by everyone who can later be held accountable to the new state. Then the various compromise devices are introduced as practical measures, and their legitimacy is derived from the legitimacy of the original contract. The assumption that unanimity creates a *de jure* state is usually not even argued for with any vigor; it seems to most democratic theorists perfectly obvious.

3. Representative Democracy

Although the problem of disagreement is the more immediate, I shall deal first with the difficulties of assembly which lead—in democratic theory—to the device of a representative parliament.[8] There are two problems which are overcome by representation: first, the total citizenry may be too numerous to meet together in a chamber or open field; and second, the business of government may require a continuous attention and application which only the idle rich or the career politician can afford to give it.

We may distinguish a number of types of representation, ranging from the mere delegation of the right to vote a proxy to a complete turning over of all decision-making functions. The question to be answered is whether any of these forms of representation adequately preserve the autonomy which men exercise through decisions taken unanimously by the entire community. In short, should a responsible man commit himself to obey the laws made by his representatives?

The simplest sort of representation is strict agency. If I am unable to attend the assembly at which votes are taken, I may turn over my proxy to an agent with instructions as to how to vote. In that case, it is obvious that I am as obligated by the decisions of the assembly as though I had been physically present. The role of legal agent is too narrowly drawn, however, to serve as an adequate model for an elected representative. In practice, it is impossible for representatives to return to their districts before each vote in the assembly and canvass their constituents. The citizens may of course arm their representative with a list of their preferences on future votes, but many of the issues which come before the assembly may not have been

8. Needless to say, the origin of parliaments historically has nothing to do with this problem. It is rather the other way around: first there were parliaments, then there was universal suffrage.

raised in the community at the time the representative was chosen. Unless there is to be a recall election on the occasion of each unforeseen deliberation, the citizens will be forced to choose as their representative a man whose general "platform" and political bent suggests that he will, in the future, vote as they imagine they would themselves, on issues which neither the citizens nor the representative yet have in mind.

When matters have reached this degree of removal from direct democracy, we may seriously doubt whether the legitimacy of the original arrangement has been preserved. I have an obligation to obey the laws which I myself enact. I have as well an obligation to obey the laws which are enacted by my agent in strict accord with my instructions. But on what grounds can it be claimed that I have an obligation to obey the laws which are made in my name by a man who has no obligation to vote as I would, who indeed has no effective way of discovering what my preferences are on the measure before him? Even if the parliament is unanimous in its adoption of some new measure, that fact can only bind the deputies and not the general citizenry who are said to be represented by them.

It can be replied that my obligation rests upon my *promise* to obey, and that may in fact be true. But insofar as a promise of that sort is the sole ground of my duty to obey, I can no longer be said to be *autonomous*. I have ceased to be the author of the laws to which I submit and have become the (willing) subject of another person. Precisely the same answer must be given to the argument that good effects of some sort will result from my obeying the duly elected parliament. The moral distinction of representative government, if there is any, does not lie in the general good which it does, nor in the fact that its subjects have consented to be ruled by a parliament. Benevolent elective kingship of a sort which has existed in past societies can say as much. The special legitimacy and moral authority of representative government is thought to result from its being an expression of the will of the people whom it rules. Representative democracy is said not simply to be government *for* the people but also government (indirectly) *by* the people. I must obey what the parliament enacts, *whatever that may be*, because its will is my will, its decisions my decisions, and hence its authority merely the collected authority of myself and my fellow citizens. Now, a parliament whose deputies vote without specific mandate from their constituents is no more the expression of their will than is a dictatorship which rules with kindly intent but independently of its subjects. It does not matter that I am pleased with the outcome after the fact, nor even that my representative has voted as he imagines I would have liked him to. So long as I do not, either in person or through my agent, join in the enactment of the laws by which I am governed, I cannot justly claim to be autonomous.

Unfounded as is traditional representative government's claim to the mantle of legitimacy, it seems impeccable in comparison with the claims of the form of "democratic" politics which actually exist in countries like the United States today. Since World War II, governments have increasingly divorced themselves in their decision-making from anything which could be called the will of the people. The complexity of the issues, the necessity of technical knowledge, and most important, the secrecy of everything having to do with national security, have conspired to attenuate the representative function of elected officials until a point has been reached which might be called political stewardship, or, after Plato, "elective guardianship." The President of the United States is merely pledged to serve the unspecified interests of his constituents in unspecified ways.

The right of such a system to the title of democracy is customarily defended by three arguments: first, the rulers are chosen by the people from a slate which includes at least two candidates for each office; second, the rulers are expected to act in what they conceive to be the interest of the people; and third, the people periodically have the opportunity to recall their rulers and select others. More generally, the system allows individuals to have some measurable influence on the ruling elite if they choose. The genealogy of the term "democracy" need not concern us. It suffices to note that the system of elective guardianship falls so far short of the ideal of autonomy and self-rule as not even to seem a distant deviation from it. Men cannot meaningfully be called free if their representatives vote independently of their wishes, or when laws are passed concerning issues which they are not able to understand. Nor can men be called free who are subject to secret decisions, based on secret data, having unannounced consequences for their well-being and their very lives.

Some while after John Kennedy was assassinated, several memoirs appeared recounting the inside story of the decisions to invade Cuba in 1961 and to risk a nuclear war by blockading Cuba in 1962. More recently, with the advent of the Nixon Administration, we have begun to learn something of the way in which President Johnson and his advisers committed this country to a massive land war in Vietnam. As this book is being prepared for publication,

75694

new decisions are being taken in secret which may involve the United States in the Laotian situation.

In none of these instances of major decisions is there the slightest relation between the real reasons determining official policy and the rationale given out for public consumption. In what way, it may be wondered, are Americans better off than those Russian subjects who were allowed, by Khrushchev's decision, to know a bit of the truth about Stalin?

Even those forms of representative government which approximate to genuine agency suffer from a curious and little-noted defect which robs electors of their freedom to determine the laws under which they shall live. The assumption which underlies the practice of representation is that the individual citizen has an opportunity, through his vote, to make his preference known. Leaving aside for the moment the problems connected with majority rule, and ignoring as well the derogations from legitimacy which result when issues are voted on in the parliament which were not canvassed during the election of deputies, the citizen who makes use of his ballot is, as it were, present in the chamber through the agency of his representative. But this assumes that at the time of the election, each man had a genuine opportunity to vote for a candidate who represented his point of view. He may find himself in the minority, of course; his candidate may lose. But at least he has had his chance to advance his preferences at the polls.

But if the number of issues under debate during the campaign is greater than one or two, and if there are—as there are sure to be—a number of plausible positions which might be taken on each issue, then the permutations of consistent alternative total "platforms" will be vastly greater than the number of candidates. Suppose, for example, that in an American election there are four issues: a farm bill, medical care for the aged, the extension of the draft, and civil rights. Simplifying the real world considerably, we can suppose that there are three alternative courses of action seriously being considered on the first issue, four on the second, two on the third, and three on the last. There are then $3 \times 4 \times 2 \times 3 = 72$ possible stands which a man might take on these four issues. For example, he might favor full parity, Kerr-Mills, discontinuation of the draft, and no civil rights bill; or free market on agricultural produce, no medicare at all, extension of the draft, and a strong civil rights bill; and so on. Now, in order to make sure that every voter has a *chance* of voting for what he believes, there would have to be 72 candidates, each holding one of the logically possible positions. If a citizen cannot even find a *candidate* whose views coincide with his own, then there is no possibility at all that he will send to the parliament a genuine *representative*. In practice, voters are offered a handful of candidates and must make compromises with their beliefs before they ever get to the polls. Under these circumstances, it is difficult to see what content there is to the platitude that elections manifest the will of the people.

The most biting rejection of representative democracy can be found in Rousseau's *Social Contract*. In opposition to such writers as Locke, Rousseau writes:

> Sovereignty cannot be represented for the same reason that it cannot be alienated; its essence is the general will, and that will must speak for itself or it does not exist: it is either itself or not itself: there is no intermediate possibility. The deputies of the people, there-

fore, are not and cannot be their representatives; they can only be their commissioners, and as such are not qualified to conclude anything. definitively. No act of theirs can be a law, unless it has been ratified by the people in person; and without that ratification nothing is a law. The people of England deceive themselves when they fancy they are free; they are so, in fact, only during the election of members of parliament: for, as soon as a new one is elected, they are again in chains, and are nothing. And thus, by the use they make of their brief moments of liberty, they deserve to lose it (Bk. III, Ch. 15).

APPENDIX: A PROPOSAL FOR INSTANT DIRECT DEMOCRACY

The practical impossibility of direct democracy is generally taken for granted in contemporary discussions of democratic theory, and it is accounted an unpleasantly utopian aspect of the philosophy of Rousseau, for example, that it assumes a community in which every citizen can vote directly on all the laws. Actually, the obstacles to direct democracy are merely technical, and we may therefore suppose that in this day of planned technological progress it is possible to solve them. The following proposal sketches one such solution. It is meant a good deal more than half in earnest, and I urge those readers who are prone to reject it out of hand to reflect on what that reaction reveals about their real attitude toward democracy.

I propose that in order to overcome the obstacles to direct democracy, a system of in-the-home voting machines be set up. In each dwelling, a device would be attached to the television set which would electronically record votes and transmit them to a computer in Washington. (Those homes without sets would be supplied by a federal subsidy. In practice this would not be very expensive, since only the very poor and the very intelligent lack sets at present.) In order to avoid fraudulent voting, the device could be rigged to record thumbprints. In that manner, each person would be able to vote only once, since the computer would automatically reject a duplicate vote. Each evening, at the time which is now devoted to news programs, there would be a nationwide all-stations show devoted to debate on the issues before the nation. Whatever bills were "before the Congress" (as we would now describe it) would be debated by representatives of alternative points of view. There would be background briefings on technically complex questions, as well as formal debates, question periods, and so forth. Committees of experts would be commissioned to gather data, make recommendations for new measures, and do the work of drafting legislation. One could institute the position of Public Dissenter in order to guarantee that dissident and unusual points of view were heard. Each Friday, after a week of debate and discussion, a voting session would be held. The measures would be put to the public, one by one, and the nation would record its preference instantaneously by means of the machines. Special arrangements might have to be made for those who could not be at their sets during the voting. (Perhaps voting sessions at various times during the preceding day and night.) Simple majority rule would prevail, as is now the case in the Congress.

The proposal is not perfect, of course, for there is a great difference between the passive role of listener in a debate and the active role of participant. Nevertheless, it should be obvious that a political community which conducted its business by means of "instant direct democracy" would be immeasurably closer to realizing the ideal of genuine democracy than we are in any so-called democratic country today. The major objection which would immediately be raised to the proposal, particularly by American political scientists, is that it would be too democratic! What chaos would ensue! What anarchy would prevail! The feckless masses, swung hither and yon by the winds of opinion, would quickly reduce the great, slow-moving, stable government of the United States to disorganized shambles! Bills would be passed or unpassed with the same casual irresponsibility which now governs the length of a hemline or the popularity of a beer. Meretricious arguments would delude the simple, well-meaning, ignorant folk into voting for pie-in-the-sky giveaways; foreign affairs would swing between jingoist militarism and craven isolationism. Gone would be the restraining hand of wisdom, knowledge, tradition, experience.

The likelihood of responses of this sort indicates the shallowness of most modern belief in democracy. It is obvious that very few individuals really hold with *government by the people*, though of course we are all willing to obliterate ourselves and our enemies in its name. Nevertheless, the unbelievers are, in my opinion, probably wrong as well as untrue to their professed faith. The initial response to a system of instant direct democracy would be chaotic, to be sure. But very quickly, men would learn— what is now manifestly not true—that their votes made a difference in the world, an immediate, visible difference. There is nothing which brings on a sense of responsibility so fast as that awareness. America would see an immediate and invigorating rise in interest in politics. It would hardly be necessary to launch expensive and frustrating campaigns to get out the vote. Politics would be on the lips of every man, woman, and child, day after day. As interest rose, a demand would be created for more and better sources of news. Even under the present system, in which very few Americans have any sense of participation in politics, news is so popular that quarter-hour programs are expanded to half an hour, and news specials preempt prime television time. Can anyone deny that instant direct democracy would generate a degree of interest and participation in political affairs which is now considered impossible to achieve?

Under a system of genuine democracy the voices of the many would drown out those of the few. The poor, the uneducated, the frightened who today are cared for by the state on occasion but never included in the process of government would weigh, man for man, as heavily as the rich, the influential, the well-connected. Much might be endangered that is worthwhile by such a system, but at least social justice would flourish as it has never flourished before.

If we are willing to think daringly, then, the practical obstacles to direct democracy can be overcome. For the moment, we need not discuss any further *whether* we wish to overcome them; but since our investigation concerns the *possibility* of establishing a state in which the autonomy of the individual is compatible with the authority of the state, I think we can take it that the difficulties which in the past have led to unsatisfactory forms of representative democracy do not constitute a serious theoretical problem.

4. Majoritarian Democracy

The principal theoretical weakness of unanimous direct democracy is its requirement that decisions be taken unanimously in order for them to acquire the authority of law. As a practical matter, of course, this requirement severely limits the actual situations in which a state can flourish, but it is perhaps an even more serious failing of unanimous democracy that it offers no way at all for men of good will to resolve their differences. Presumably, in order for the concept of a just state to have more than idle interest, it must at least in theory be possible for conflicts to be resolved without a loss of autonomy on the part of the citizens or of authority on the part of the state. The conflicts need not be motivated by divisive self-interest; they may simply be disagreements over the best way to pursue the common good.

The solution which immediately springs to the fore is, of course, majority rule. Where the electorate are divided, take a vote; give to each man one vote, and let the group as a whole be committed by the preponderance of voices. So widespread is the belief in majority rule that there is not a single variant of democratic theory which does not call upon it as the means for composing differences and arriving at decisions. Our task is to discover an argument which demonstrates that the autonomy of unanimous democracy is preserved in a democracy which is guided by the rule of the majority. In other words, we must inquire whether the members of a democratic polity are morally bound to obey the decisions of the majority, and if so, why.

The problem, of course, concerns those who find themselves in the minority on any question. The members of
the majority bear the same relation to the law they have
passed as do all the citizens in a unanimous democracy.
Since the majority have willed the law, they are bound by
it, and they remain autonomous in submitting to its authority. A member of the minority, however, has voted
against the law, and he appears to be in the position of a
man who, deliberating on a moral question, rejects an
alternative only to find it forced upon him by a superior
power. His readiness to deliberate, and to be committed
by his decision, manifests his desire to be autonomous; but
insofar as he must submit to the will of the majority, it
seems that his desire is frustrated.

One common justification of majority rule is that, on
prudential or general moral grounds, it works better than
any other system which has been devised. For example, it
is said that democratic politics is a substitute for the rule
of arms which prevails in lawless societies. Since the majority are, militarily speaking, likely to be the superior
body, they must be allowed to rule by the ballot; for otherwise they will resort to force and throw society back into
chaos. Or, again, historical observation may reveal that
rule by the majority tends to advance the general welfare
better than any other system of government (such as rule
by the wise or the powerful), since contrary to what Plato
and others have supposed, the people know their own interest best. Majoritarian democracy, it is said, is therefore
the most effective safeguard against the rule of a hypo-
critically self-interested elite. From the point of view of
the individual, it might be urged that submission to the
rule of the majority offers him the best chance, in the long

run, for advancing his own interests, since by and large he will find himself in the majority as often as in the minority, and the benefit flowing from collective action will outweigh the losses suffered when his side loses.

All such defenses, and others besides which might be based on considerations of interest or good consequences, are, however, strictly irrelevant to our inquiry. As justifications for an individual's autonomous decision to cooperate with the state, they may be perfectly adequate; but as demonstrations of the *authority* of the state—as proofs, that is, of the right of the state to command the individual and of his obligation to obey, *whatever may be commanded*—they fail completely. If the individual retains his autonomy by reserving to himself in each instance the final decision whether to cooperate, he thereby denies the authority of the state; if, on the other hand, he submits to the state and accepts its claim to authority, then so far as any of the above arguments indicate, he loses his autonomy.

Indeed, the prudential and casuistical defenses of democracy do not succeed in distinguishing it morally from any other form of political community. A man might find that his affairs flourished in a dictatorship or monarchy, and even that the welfare of the people as a whole was effectively advanced by the policies of such a state. Democracy, then, could claim to be no more than one type of *de facto* government among many, and its virtues, if any, would be purely relative. Perhaps, as Winston Churchill once remarked, democracy is the worst form of government except for all the others; but if so, then the "citizens" of America are as much subjects of an alien power as the Spaniards under Franco or the Russians under Stalin. They are merely more fortunate in their rulers.

A more serious case for majority rule can be founded on the terms of the contract by which the political order is constituted. According to many theorists of democracy, the transition from unanimous rule, as exemplified by the adoption of the social contract, to majority rule, on which the subsequent functionings of the society depend, is provided for by a clause in the original agreement. Everyone pledges himself henceforth to abide by the rule of the majority, and whenever a citizen objects to being required to obey laws for which he has not voted, he can be recalled to his promise. On that pact, it is asserted, rests the moral authority of a majoritarian state.[9]

But this argument is no better than the previous one. A promise to abide by the will of the majority creates an obligation, *but it does so precisely by giving up one's autonomy.* It is perfectly possible to forfeit autonomy, as we have already seen. Whether it is wise, or good, or right to do so is, of course, open to question, but *that* one can do so is obvious. Hence, if citizens contract to govern themselves by majority rule, they thereby obligate themselves in just

9. A great deal has been written, in mitigation of the manifest historical implausibility of contract theories, about the metaphorical or mythical character of the original "contract." Sometimes, for example, it is said that the contract merely states in convenient form the underlying moral consensus of the society. It should be clear that a sophisticated interpretation of this sort will not do, if one wishes to found majority rule on the promise contained in the contract. A promise is an act, not the mere expression or summation of an existing obligation. It creates a new obligation where none existed before. Whatever may be my general moral obligation to do an act, my promise to do it lays an independent burden of responsibility upon me. Hence, those theorists who trace the legitimacy of majoritarianism to the contract cannot, in all consistency, dissolve the contract into a myth. Needless to say, there can be tacit promises as well as explicit promises, and therefore tacit or quasi-contracts of the sort which are invoked to explain the obligation of succeeding generations.

the manner that they would be obligated by any promise. The state then has a right to command them, assuming that it is guided only by the majority. But the citizens have created a legitimate state at the price of their own autonomy! They have bound themselves to obey laws which they do not will, and indeed even laws which they vigorously reject. Insofar as democracy originates in such a promise, it is no more than voluntary slavery, and the characterization which Rousseau gives of the English form of representation can as well be applied here.

The force of this point is difficult to grasp, for we are so deeply imbued with the ethic of majoritarianism that it possesses for us the deceptive quality of self-evidence. In the United States, little children are taught to let the majority rule almost before they are old enough to count the votes. Whenever force or wealth threatens to dominate a situation, the voice of the majority is appealed to as the higher call of morality and reason. Not rule by the majority? What else is there, one wants to ask. Perhaps it will help, therefore, to reflect that the justification of majority rule by appeal to an original promise opens the way to justification of virtually any other mode of decision-making, for the contracting citizens could as well have promised to abide by minority rule, or random choice, or the rule of a monarch, or rule by the best educated, or rule by the least educated, or even rule by a daily dictator chosen by lot.

If the only argument for majority rule is its legitimation by unanimous vote at the founding convention, then presumably *any* method of decision-making at all which was given that sanction would be equally legitimate. If we hold that majority rule has some special validity, then it must be because of the character of majority rule itself, and not because of a promise which we may be thought to have made to abide by it. What is required, therefore, is a direct justification of majority rule itself, that is, a demonstration that under majority rule the minority do not forfeit their autonomy in submitting to the decisions of the collectivity.

John Locke somewhat recognizes the necessity for a proof of the principle of majority rule, and at the very outset of his *Second Treatise Concerning Civil Government* offers the following:

> When any number of men have so consented to make one community or government, they are thereby presently incorporated, and make one body politic, wherein the majority have a right to act and conclude the rest. For when any number of men have, by the consent of every individual, made a community, they have thereby made that community one body, with a power to act as one body, which is only by the will and determination of the majority. For that which acts [i.e., activates] any community being only the consent of the individuals of it, and it being one body must move one way, it is necessary the body should move that way whither the greater force carries it, which is the consent of the majority; or else it is impossible it should act or continue one body, one community, which the consent of every individual that united into it agreed that it should; and so every one is bound by that consent to be concluded by the majority (Ch. VIII).

The key to the argument is the assertion that the body politic must be carried "whither the greater force carries it." If this means that the state *must in fact* move in the direction of the preponderance of power, it is either trivially true, power being defined by its effects, or else nontrivial and false, since frequently a minority can dominate the conduct of public affairs even though they command far less than a preponderance of the available force in the society. On the other hand, if Locke means that the state *ought* to move in the direction of the greater *moral* force, then presumably he believes that the majority will possess that superior moral force because each individual counts for one in the moral calculus. However, even if sense can be made of the notion of a moral force, we are still without a reason why the minority has an obligation to obey the majority.

One possible line of argument is to found the rule of the majority on the higher principle that each person in the society should have an equal chance to make his preferences the law. Assuming for the moment that the principle of equal chance is valid, does majority rule achieve that equality?

It is difficult to decide, since the notion of having an equal chance of making one's preferences law is ambiguous. In one sense, majority rule *guarantees* to the members of the majority that their preference will become law. Hence if a man knows that he is in the minority, he will realize that he has *no* chance at all of effecting his will. This is the characteristic of majoritarian democracy which drives permanent minorities into rebellion, and permits what Mill quite justly called the tyranny of the majority. A system of legislation by lot might therefore be more in accord with the principle of equal chance. Each individual could write his preference on a piece of paper, and the winning law could be drawn from a twirling basket. Then, we might suppose, each citizen could have exactly the same chance that his will would become law. But probability is a tricky science, and here again we must pause to reconsider. Each citizen, to be sure, would have the same chance for his piece of paper to be drawn from the basket; but presumably what he desires is simply that the law which he prefers be enacted, not that the enactment take place by means of his personal slip of paper. In other words, he would be equally satisfied by a drawing of *any* piece of paper on which his preference was written. Now, if there are more slips with alternative A on them than with alternative B, then of course the probability is higher of alternative A being chosen. Thus, legislation by lot would offer some chance to the minority, unlike rule by the majority, but it would not offer to each citizen an equal chance that his preference be enacted. Nevertheless, it does seem to come closer to the ideal of equal chances than majority rule.

We have cited the device of decision by random choice chiefly as a way of exposing the weaknesses of a certain justification of majority rule, but before going on to yet another argument for majoritarianism, it might be well to consider whether random decision is a worthy candidate for adoption in its own right. Is it reasonable to resolve differences of opinion by chance? Does commitment to such a device preserve the autonomy of the individual citizen, even when the die is cast against him?

We must not be too hasty in rejecting the appeal to chance, for in at least some situations of choice it would appear to be the proper method. For example, if I am faced with a choice among alternatives whose probable outcomes I cannot estimate, then it is perfectly sensible to let chance decide my choice. If I am lost in the forest, with not the slightest idea which direction is most promising, and if I am convinced that my best chance is to choose one path and stick to it, then I might as well spin myself around with my eyes closed and start off in any direction. More generally, it is reasonable to choose at random among equally promising alternatives.[10] Random decision is also reasonable in another sort of case, where rewards or burdens are to be distributed among equally deserving (or undeserving) citizens, and the nature of the item to be distributed makes it impossible to divide it and parcel out equal shares. Thus, if the armed forces require only one-half of the available men, and cannot adjust matters by halving the service time and doubling the draft, then the fair method of choosing inductees is to put the names in a bowl and pull them out at random.

Since the duty of autonomy dictates only that I use all *available* information in making my decisions, it is clear that randomization in the face of ignorance is not a derogation of autonomy. This is equally true in the second case, of indivisible payoffs, though we are there obligated to attempt to overcome the inevitable unfairness by incorporating the matter into a broader context and balancing off future rewards and burdens. It follows that the use of ran-

10. I am deliberately glossing over the much more controversial question, whether it is reasonable to equate a less probable outcome having a high value to me with a more probable outcome having a low value. Somewhat more technically, the question is whether I ought to be guided by my calculation of the expected value, or mathematical expectation, of the alternatives open to me. Von Neumann and Morgenstern, in their development of the pure theory of games, assume the rationality of maximization of expected value, but there is nothing approaching consensus on the issue in the contemporary literature.

dom devices in some collective decision will not violate autonomy, assuming for the moment that there has been unanimous agreement on their adoption. But what shall we say of the decision by lot in cases where the obstacle to decision is simple disagreement among the members of the assembly, and not ignorance of future outcomes or the indivisibility of payoffs? Is this, perhaps, a solution to the problem of the subjection of the minority?

In the making of individual decisions, an appeal to chance when the necessary information was at hand would be a willful forfeiture of autonomy. May we then conclude that the same is true for collective decision? Not so, it might be argued. If we are permitted, without loss of autonomy, to bow to the constraints of ignorance, or to the intractability of nature, why may we not with equal justification adjust ourselves to the limitations of collective as opposed to individual decision-making? When the assembly of the people cannot reach a unanimous decision, decision by lot is the only way to avoid the twin evils of governmental inertia and tyrannization of the minority.

This argument seems to me to be wrong, although my reasons for this belief will only be spelled out with any fullness in the last section of this essay. Briefly, there is a fundamental difference between those obstacles to decision which are outside our control, such as ignorance, and those obstacles which are at least theoretically within our control, such as psychological conflict (in the individual) or disagreement (in the society as a whole). Whereas we have no reason to think that we could ever completely overcome natural obstacles, even in an ideal society, we must suppose that some method exists for resolving conflicts among rational men of good will which allows them to concert their activities without forfeiting their autonomy. The general adoption of decision by lot would violate the autonomy of the citizens.

The most ambitious defense of majoritarianism in the literature of democratic theory is that offered by Jean-Jacques Rousseau in Book IV of the *Social Contract*. The fundamental problem of political philosophy, according to Rousseau, is to discover whether there is "a form of association which will defend and protect with the whole common force the person and the property of each associate, and by which every person, while uniting himself with all, shall obey only himself and remain as free as before."[11] The solution to this problem is the social contract by which men first constitute themselves a polity. By means of the contract, the many particular and divisive wills of the prepolitical community are transformed into the general will of the collective body. Each contracting party pledges himself to "place in common his person and all his power under the supreme direction of the general will; and as one body ... all receive each member as an indivisible part of the whole."

A will is distinguished by Rousseau as general by virtue both of its form and of its content, or aim. Formally, a will is general insofar as it issues in commands having the form of general law rather than particular edict. Thus, Rousseau considers only the laws of the society to be products of the general will; applications of the laws to particular

11. This is essentially the problem which I have called the deduction of the possibility of political philosophy. Rousseau appears to be the first political philosopher to recognize explicitly the conflict between the demands of moral autonomy and legitimate authority. My treatment of the problem owes a great deal to the *Social Contract*. (Bk. I, Ch. VI)

cases are made by the government, which operates under a mandate from the collective will of the people. Materially, a will is general insofar as it aims at the general good rather than at the particular goods of separate individuals. An individual can be said to have a general will, or to strive for a general will, if he aims at the general good rather than his own good, and if he issues commands having the form of law. Similarly, the group as a whole has a general will when it issues laws which aim at the general good. In this way, Rousseau distinguishes a true political community from an association of self-interested individuals who strike bargains among their competing interests, but nowhere strive for the good of the whole. (The same distinction is said to be embodied in the division of function between the Congress, which represents sectional and class interests, and the president, who is supposed to be guided by the national interest.)

It is Rousseau's claim that when a political community deliberates together on the general good and embodies its deliberations in general laws, it thereby acquires legitimate authority over all the members of the deliberating body, or parliament. Thenceforward, each member of the society has a moral obligation to obey the laws which have been willed by the collectivity. That obligation can be suspended only when the general will is destroyed, which is to say only if the parliament of all the people ceases to aim at the general good or to issue laws.

Rousseau, in keeping with the tradition of democratic theory, introduces the device of majority rule into the founding contract. But he recognizes that the legitimacy of laws enacted by a majority of the parliament cannot be traced merely to the binding force of a promise. In

Book IV of the *Social Contract,* therefore, he returns to the problem:

> Except in this original contract, a majority of the votes is sufficient to bind all the others. This is a consequence of the contract itself. But it may be asked how a man can be free and yet forced to conform to the will of others. How are the opposers free when they are in submission to laws to which they have never consented?

Rousseau continues:

> I answer that the question is not fairly stated. The citizen consents to all the laws, to those which are passed in spite of his opposition, and even to those which sentence him to punishment if he violates any one of them. The constant will of all the members of the State is the general will; it is by that they are citizens and free. When any law is proposed to the assembly of the people, the question is not precisely to enquire whether they approve the proposition or reject it, but if it is conformable or not to the general will, which is their will. Each citizen, in giving his suffrage, states his mind on that question; and the general will is found by counting the votes. When, therefore, the motion which I opposed carries, it only proves to me that I was mistaken, and that what I believed to be the general will was not so. If my particular opinion had prevailed, I should have done what I was not willing to do, and consequently, I should not have been in a state of freedom.

The air of paradox which surrounds this passage has enticed or repelled students of Rousseau ever since the *Social Contract* appeared. The notion of man being "forced to be free," which was employed by later idealist political philosophers to justify the state's repression of the individual "in the interest of his own true self," can be traced to this argument. Actually, as I shall try to show, there are no sinister implications to Rousseau's argument, although it is not valid.

The foundation of the argument is a distinction, whose lineage runs at least to Plato, between doing what one wills and doing what one wants. An individual may be said to do what he wills so long as he manages to perform the action which he sets out to perform; but he may thereby fail to do what he wants, if the outcome of the action is other than he anticipated. For example, suppose that I arrive at a train station just as my train is scheduled to leave. Not knowing which track I am to leave from, I rush up to a conductor and shout, "Which track for Boston?" He points at track 6, but I misunderstand him and dash off for track 5, where a train for Philadelphia is also on the point of leaving. The conductor, seeing my mistake, has only two choices: he can allow me to board the wrong train, thereby permitting me to do what I will, or bodily hustle me onto the right train, thereby forcing me to do what I want. Rousseau's description seems perfectly apposite. If the conductor makes no move to stop me, I will fail to do what I want to do, and in that sense not be free.

Consider another case, that of an intern who is on duty in the emergency ward of a hospital. A case comes in which he misdiagnoses as poisoning. He orders a stomach pump, which is about to be applied when the resident in charge happens by, recognizes the case as actually one of appendicitis, for which the stomach pump would be fatal, and countermands the intern's order to the nurse. Here, the intern's aim is of course to cure the patient, and he is assisted in achieving it by the resident's counterorder, which (in a manner of speaking) forces him to treat the patient correctly. Had he been permitted to follow his own diagnosis, he would have accomplished precisely the end which he most wished to avoid.

Plato, it will be recalled, uses this same argument in the *Gorgias* and *Republic* in order to demonstrate that the tyrant is not truly powerful. The tyrant, like all men, wants what is good for him. Power, then, is the ability to get what is good for oneself. But the tyrant, through a defect of true moral knowledge, mistakenly thinks that it is good for him to indulge his appetites, deal unjustly with his fellow men, and subordinate his rational faculties to his unchecked desire and will. As a result, he becomes what we would today call a neurotic individual; he compulsively pursues fantasy-goals whose achievement gives him no real happiness, and he thereby shows himself to be truly powerless to get what he wants.

The three cases of the man catching a train, the intern diagnosing a patient, and the tyrant have three common characteristics on which are founded the distinction between getting what one wills and getting what one wants. First, it is supposedly quite easy to distinguish between the goal of the individual's action and the means which he adopts to achieve it. (This is, of course, debatable in the case of the tyrant; it would hardly be denied in the other cases.) Hence, we can speak meaningfully of the agent's willing the means and wanting the end, and therefore of his doing what he wills but failing to get what he wants. Second, the goal in each case is some state of affairs whose existence is objectively ascertainable, and about which one can have knowledge. (Again, Plato's example is open to dispute; this is precisely the point in the development of his ethical theory at which he makes use of the doctrine that there is such a thing as moral knowledge.) It follows that a man may sometimes know less well what he really wants (i.e., what will really accomplish his own goals) than some independent observer. Finally, in all three cases we are to assume that the individual places a purely instrumental value on the means which he adopts, and would be willing to give them up if he believed that they were ill suited to his ends.

Life is full of significant situations in which we strive to achieve some objective state of affairs, and in which we would therefore be sorry if our mistaken views about the means to those ends were to be adopted. For example, if a member of Congress genuinely wishes to reduce unemployment, and if his traditionalistic convictions about the virtues of a balanced budget are overriden by a liberal majority which seeks to spend the nation into prosperity, *and if unemployment is thereupon reduced,* then (personal pride to one side) we may expect him to be glad that his views were in the minority, for he can now see that "if his particular opinion had prevailed, he should have done what he was not willing to do, and consequently, he should not have been in a state of freedom."

And we can now see what Rousseau intended in the passage quoted above. He assumes that the assembly of the people is attempting to issue commands which have the form of law and aim at the general good. This is a legitimate assumption for Rousseau to make, since he is only interested in discovering whether a community which *does* aim at the general good thereby confers legitimacy on the laws which it passes. The further question, whether one can often find an assembly which holds to the ideal of the general good instead of pursuing diverse particular interests, concerns the application of Rousseau's theory. Democratic theorists frequently devote great attention to the problem of devising safeguards against the ineradicable partisanship of even the most enlightened men. Although that is indeed a serious matter, their concern tends to mask their unexamined assumption that a majoritarian democracy of thoroughly public-spirited citizens, if it ever could exist, would possess legitimate authority. This is merely one more reflection of the universal conviction that majority rule is self-evidently legitimate. By recognizing the necessity for an independent justification of majority rule, Rousseau plays in political philosophy the role which Hume plays in the theory of knowledge.

Rousseau supposes further that it is an objectively ascertainable fact whether a proposed law has the proper form and aims at the general good. He thinks, finally, that the proper test of these matters is a vote, in which the majority must inevitably be correct. Hence, when a member of the assembly "gives his suffrage," he is not expressing his *preference*, but rather offering his opinion on the character of the proposed law. He may perfectly well prefer a different measure, which serves his interest better, and nevertheless vote for the proposal because he believes it to aim at the general good. Since the majority are always right, a member of the minority will *by that fact* be revealed as supporting inappropriate means to his own end; in short, the minority are like the individual who dashes for the wrong train, or the intern who prescribes the wrong treatment.

The flaw in this argument, of course, is the apparently

groundless assumption that the majority are always right in their opinion concerning the general good. (Rousseau's appeal to this assumption is contained in the innocuous-looking words "and the general will is found by counting the votes.") What can possibly have led Rousseau to such an implausible conclusion? Experience would seem rather to suggest that truth lies with the minority in most disputes, and certainly that is the case in the early stages of the acceptance of new discoveries. At any rate, if the nature of the general good is a matter of knowledge, then there would appear to be no ground for assuming that the majority opinion on any particular proposal for the general good will inevitably be correct.

I think we can trace Rousseau's error to a pair of complicated confusions. First, Rousseau has not adequately distinguished between an assembly which attempts to aim at the general good, and one which actually succeeds. In a chapter entitled "Whether the General Will Can Err," he writes:

> It follows from what has been said that the general will is always right and tends always to the public advantage; but it does not follow that the deliberations of the people have always the same rectitude. Our will always seeks our own good, but we do not always perceive what it is. The people are never corrupted, but they are often deceived, and only then do they seem to will what is bad. (Bk. I, Ch. 3)

The confusion lies in failing to distinguish three possible conditions of the assembly. First, the citizenry may vote on the basis of private interest, in which case they are not even attempting to realize the general good. That is what

Rousseau calls an "aggregate will." Second, the people may strive to achieve the general good, but choose poor laws because of their ignorance, or simply the unpredictability of important aspects of the problems which they face. Insofar as everyone does his best to realize the general good, the collectivity is a genuine moral and political community. Finally, the assembly of the people may aim at the general good and hit it. They may deliberately choose to enact laws which do in fact offer the best way to achieve the good of the community.

Now, there may be some ground for claiming that an assembly which is in the second condition has legitimate authority over its members; one might argue that it acquires authority by virtue of the universal commitment of its members to the general good. But Rousseau's proof of the legitimacy of the majority will only work if we assume that the assembly is in the third condition—that whenever it is guided by the majority it actually succeeds in moving toward the general good. In that case, it really would be true that a member of the minority could get what he willed (the general good) only by failing to get what he voted for.

The confusion between trying to achieve the general good and succeeding is compounded, I would like to suggest, by a second confusion which leads Rousseau to overlook what would otherwise be a rather obvious error. There are three questions which one might suppose the assembly to be presented with. Rousseau mentions two: Which law do you prefer? and Which law tends to the general good? A third question might also be asked: Which alternative will win? Now the peculiarity of this last question is that the majority opinion *must be correct.* If everyone's vote is a prediction about the outcome, then the members of the minority will hardly desire their choice to prevail, for by so doing they would violate the principle of majority rule to which they are presumably committed. The phrase "general will" is ambiguous in Rousseau's usage, even though he takes great care to define it earlier in his essay. It should mean "will issuing laws which aim at the general good," but it frequently has for him the more ordinary meaning "preponderant opinion" or "consensus of the group." When the assembly is asked "whether (the proposition before them) is conformable or not to the general will," we may view them either as being asked for their opinion of the value of the proposition for the general good, or else as being asked to make a prediction of the outcome of the vote. I suggest that Rousseau himself confused these two senses, and was thereby led into the manifestly false assumption that the majority opinion of the assembly would successfully express what the minority were really striving for, and hence be binding on everyone who voted for or against.

We appear to be left with no plausible reason for believing that a direct democracy governed by majority rule preserves the moral autonomy of the individual while conferring legitimate authority on the sovereign. The problem remains, that those who submit to laws against which they have voted are no longer autonomous, even though they may have submitted voluntarily. The strongest argument for the moral authority of a majoritarian government is that it is founded upon the unanimous promise of obedience of its subjects. If such a promise may be supposed to exist, then the government does indeed have a moral right to command. But we have discovered no *moral* reason why men should by their promise bring a democratic state into being, and thereby forfeit their autonomy. The implicit claim of all democratic theory, I repeat, is that it offers a solution to the problem of combining moral liberty (autonomy) with political authority. This claim is justified for the special case of unanimous direct democracy. But none of the arguments which we have considered thus far succeed in demonstrating that this claim is also valid for majoritarian democracy.

This is not to deny that there are many other reasons for favoring democracy of one sort or another under the conditions which prevail today in advanced industrial societies. For example, one might reply impatiently to all the foregoing argumentation that majority rule seems to work well enough, and that minorities do not show signs of feeling trampled upon, for all that they may be frustrated or disappointed. To which one need only reply that the psychology of politics is not at issue here. Men's feelings of loss of autonomy, like their feelings of loyalty, are determined by such factors as the relative degree of satisfaction and frustration of deeply held desires which they experience. Modern interest-group democracy is, under some circumstances, an effective means of reducing frustrations, or at least of reducing the connection between frustration and political disaffection. But many other forms of political organization might accomplish this result, such as benevolent autocracy or charismatic dictatorship. If democracy is to make good its title as the only morally legitimate form of politics, then it must solve the problem of the heteronomous minority.

APPENDIX: THE IRRATIONALITY OF MAJORITY RULE

Majority rule can be called into question on grounds of its failure to preserve the liberty of the minority, but it has commonly been thought to be at least a rational method of making decisions, supposing that the members of the community are willing to agree upon its adoption. In fact it turns out that majority rule is fatally flawed by an internal inconsistency which ought to disqualify it from consideration in any political community whatsoever.

Self-consistency is perhaps the simplest sort of rationality which is demanded of all men in their deliberations and actions. If a man prefers a first state of affairs or action to a second, and prefers the second in turn to a third, then in all consistency he ought to prefer the first to the third. There is of course no psychological law which forces a man to keep his preferences consistent, any more than to adopt only means which he believes are well suited to his ends. But in exploring the theoretical possibility of a legitimate state, we are surely justified in positing a community of citizens who rise to that first level of rationality.

Presumably, also, we desire that the method of group decision which we adopt will lead to collective action having the like virtue of internal consistency. Unanimous democracy achieves this end, for it reproduces in the laws of the state the common preferences of the entire citizenry. If their preferences are consistent, so too will be those of the state. It might be thought that majority rule also preserved consistency of preference, but the facts are otherwise. As a simple example will illustrate, it is perfectly possible for a group of rational individuals with consistent preferences to arrive, by majority rule, at a completely inconsistent order of group preference! Suppose for the sake of simplicity that the community consists of three individuals who are faced with the problem of establishing a social ranking among three alternatives.[12] Each member of the voting community is first asked to rank the three possibilities in order of his relative preference. He may use any criteria he chooses—such as social utility, personal interest, or even whim—but he must be consistent. The group then establishes its collective preference by voting for the alternatives, two at a time. Since there are three alternatives, which we can call A, B, and C, there will be three votes in all: first A against B, then A against C, and finally B against C.

The preference order of the society is completely determined by the preference orders of the individuals, for whenever a pair of alternatives is presented to them, each man consults his private ranking and votes for the higher of the two. Now, there are a great many possible sets of private orderings which, when amalgamated by the device of majority rule, will produce a consistent public ordering. For example, consider the set of orderings in Table 1.

Table 1.

Individual I	Individual II	Individual III
A	A	B
C	B	C
B	C	A

Since Individuals I and II prefer A to B, they outvote Individual III, and the society as a whole prefers A to B. Simi-

12. The paradox, or inconsistency, which is developed in the text may be duplicated in any case involving two or more voters and three or more alternatives, assuming that one is permitted to be indifferent between any pair of alternatives, as well as to prefer one to the other. The "voter's paradox," as it is called, has been known for some time, and was actually the subject of an extended treatise by the nineteenth-century mathematician Charles Dodgson, better known as Lewis Carroll.

larly, Individuals II and III outvote Individual I and commit the society to B over C. Now, if the society prefers A to B, and B to C, then in all consistency, it ought also to prefer A to C. And so indeed it does, for Individuals I and II vote that preference, and thereby overrule Individual III once more. In this case, majority rule has transformed a consistent set of individual or private preference rankings into an equally consistent social preference ranking. But unfortunately, it is not always so.

Consider the set of individual orderings of the same alternatives in Table 2.

Table 2.

Individual I	Individual II	Individual III
A	B	C
B	C	A
C	A	B

When we pair the alternatives and count the votes, we discover that there is a majority for A over B (Individuals I and II), and a majority for B over C (Individuals I and II), but *not* therefore a majority for A over C. Quite to the contrary, Individuals II and III prefer C to A, and therefore so does the society. The result is that the group as a whole, starting from perfectly consistent individual preferences, has arrived by majority rule at an absurdly inconsistent group preference.

It might be objected that we have presented a false picture of rule by the majority. Assemblies do not vote on all the pair-wise combinations of possibilities which are under consideration. They either vote for all at once, and allow a plurality to decide, or else they take measures up one at a time, adopting or rejecting them. It makes no difference. The contradictions which we have discovered in majority voting can be reproduced in any of the ordinary variations which might be adopted by an assembly. For example, suppose that the procedure is followed of voting on the alternatives one at a time, until one is adopted, which thereupon becomes law. Each citizen votes against a proposal if there is some alternative still in the running which he prefers. On the other hand, once a proposal has been voted down, it is eliminated from the contest and is ignored by the electorate. Under this system, one can easily show that the winning measure is determined (in the paradoxical case outlined above) solely by the order in which the possibilities are brought before the voters. To see that this is true, consider once more the pattern of preferences exhibited in Table 2. There are three alternatives, A, B, and C. Hence there are six different orders in which the alternatives can be presented to the assembly, namely ABC, ACB, BAC, BCA, CAB, and CBA. Let us see what happens in each case under the system of eliminative voting.

Case 1.   A is put before the assembly and loses, since two individuals prefer something else to it.

B is now put before the assembly and wins, for with A eliminated, there are now two individuals who prefer it to anything else (i.e., to C), and only one who still has a prior preference for C.

So B wins.

Case 2.   A is put before the assembly and loses; C is put before the assembly and also loses; leaving B, which wins.

Case 3.   By the same line of reasoning, when B is put before the assembly it loses; whereupon A also loses, leaving C, which wins.

Case 4.   B loses; C wins.

Case 5.   Starting with C, which loses, we end up with A, which wins.

Case 6.   A wins.

In short, when alternative A is voted on first, alternative B wins; when alternative B is voted on first, alternative C wins; and when alternative C is voted on first, alternative A wins. It is clearly irrational for a society to change its preference among three alternatives whenever it considers them in a different order. That would be like saying that I prefer chocolate ice cream to vanilla when I am offered chocolate first, but prefer vanilla to chocolate when I am offered vanilla first!

Kenneth Arrow, in an important monograph entitled *Social Choice and Individual Values,* has demonstrated that the inconsistency of the voter's paradox infects virtually every method of social choice which can lay a reasonable claim to being called "democratic." How can it be that when rational men with consistent preferences make collective decisions by the apparently legitimate device of majority rule, they may arrive at inconsistent group preferences? What is it about the process of collective decision which introduces an element of irrationality?

The answer seems to be contained in a very interesting discovery of Duncan Black concerning the conditions under which majority rule can be trusted to yield consistent results. It is obvious that we can guarantee the consistency of majority rule if we are permitted to set limits to the patterns of individual preference which the voters may adopt. In the extreme case, for example, if we require everyone to adopt the *same* preference order, then of course majority rule will simply reproduce that order as the social preference, which will be consistent. But are there any *reasonable* restrictions that will do the job? And, further, what is the weakest restriction that will ensure a consistent social preference order? The answer to the latter question is not yet known, but Black has demonstrated that under one interesting and natural restriction, majority rule will work consistently.

Briefly, the restriction is that every individual's preference order must exhibit the characteristic which he calls "single-peakedness" when plotted on a single scale. This means that there is some one-dimensional array of all the alternatives, on which each individual can locate his first choice, and which has the property that for every individual, the farther to the right an alternative is from his first choice, the less he prefers it, and the farther to the left an alternative is from his first choice, the less he prefers it. We are all familiar with such an array, namely the "left-right" spectrum in politics. If we string out the various political positions on the spectrum from extreme left, or radical, to extreme right, or reactionary, then the following is true: First, each individual can locate himself along the spectrum; Second, once he has found his place, which is the position of his first choice, then the farther to the right or left something is, the less he likes it.[13] For ex-

13. But notice, nothing can be said about his relative preferences among one position to the right and another to the left. This is because the ordering of his preference is ordinal, not cardinal.

ample, a moderate Republican prefers a conservative to a radical, and he also prefers a liberal Republican to a moderate Democrat. A left-wing Democrat prefers a socialist to a Communist, and also a middle-of-the-road Democrat to an Eisenhower Republican. And so forth. Black has demonstrated mathematically that if every person can satisfactorily fit his preferences onto such a spectrum, then majority rule must give a consistent social preference.

It is not completely clear what the deeper significance is of Black's discovery. One clue seems to be that single-peakedness, or arrangement along a left-right spectrum, occurs when everyone in the society views the alternatives as embodying varying degrees of some one magnitude. This is roughly akin to Aristotle's notion of virtue as a mean between extremes. Each virtue is seen as occupying a position on a scale, midway (roughly) between an excess and a defect. For example, courage is analyzed as a mean between rashness and cowardice. Presumably, the further one errs toward the direction of either extreme, the worse one is. In politics, we might interpret the left-right spectrum as a reflection of varying degrees of government intervention in social questions. At one end are the conservatives, who desire minimum intervention; at the other end are the socialists, who desire maximum intervention; and strung out between the two are various types of moderates who favor a mixture of intervention and nonintervention.[14]

When a single individual evaluates alternatives, the vari-

14. Notice that in this case, the conservatives and socialists do not focus their attention upon the same variable, but rather on two different variables which may be supposed to vary together. The conservatives are concerned with intervention *per se*, but the socialists are presumably concerned with social welfare and social justice, which they believe varies directly with the degree of intervention.

able or variables with which he is concerned presumably remain the same throughout his evaluation. This is one of the sources of his internal consistency. But when many individuals evaluate the same objective alternatives, they may do so in terms of a diversity of variables. The result is that when their decisions are collectively amalgamated through voting, the group preference may embody the inconsistency of standards of evaluation which existed, in a disaggregated form, in the voting population. It would seem, therefore, that majority rule has the best chance of yielding consistent results when the entire citizenry views the issues as polarized, in terms of variables which make it natural to prefer alternatives less and less as they diverge, in either direction, from one's first choice.

In order to see how lack of single-peakedness can lead to inconsistency, let us take a look at a simplified society in which there are three voters, a conservative, a welfare-state liberal, and a socialist, who must choose among three alternatives, namely laissez-faire capitalism, welfare-state liberalism, and socialism. The conservative, we may assume, would prefer laissez faire first, welfare-state liberalism second, and socialism last. It is also plausible that the liberal would prefer welfare-state liberalism first, socialism second, and laissez-faire capitalism last. But the socialist, who locates himself at the extreme left of the political spectrum, and prefers socialism first, might *not* prefer the welfare state second. He might in fact think that the welfare state had the worst features of both laissez-faire capitalism and socialism, with the virtues of neither. The welfare state throttles individual initiative, which does after all have a number of socially desirable consequences under capitalism, while also laying upon the society the burden of bureaucracy devoid of the rational total control possible under socialism. The socialist's preference order might therefore read socialism first, laissez faire second, and the welfare state last. Table 3 summarizes these individual preference orders:

Table 3.

Conservative	Liberal	Socialist
laissez faire	welfare state	socialism
welfare state	socialism	laissez faire
socialism	laissez faire	welfare state

What would be the result of a vote? The society would prefer laissez faire to the welfare state, two-to-one; it would also prefer the welfare state to socialism, two-to-one. But it would *not* prefer laissez faire to socialism. Quite to the contrary, by a vote of 2 to 1 it would prefer socialism to laissez faire. Thus even when the members of a voting assembly see the alternatives as embodying varying degrees of a single magnitude (state control), there may still not be a single-peakedness, and hence no consistency in the group preference.

III.
Beyond the
Legitimate State

1. The Quest for the Legitimate State

We have come to a dead end in our search for a viable form of political association which will harmonize the moral autonomy of the individual with the legitimate authority of the state. The one proposal which appears genuinely to resolve the conflict, namely unanimous direct democracy, is so restricted in its application that it offers no serious hope of ever being embodied in an actual state. Indeed, since it achieves its success only by ruling out precisely the conflicts of opinion which politics is designed to resolve, it may be viewed as the limiting case of a solution rather than as itself a true example of a legitimate state.

A contractual democracy is legitimate, to be sure, for it is founded upon the citizens' promise to obey its commands. Indeed, any state is legitimate which is founded upon such a promise. However, all such states achieve their legitimacy only by means of the citizens' forfeit of their autonomy, and hence are not solutions to the fundamental problem of political philosophy. Majoritarian democracy claims a deeper justification than merely an original promise. It presents itself as the only viable form of political community in which the citizenry rule themselves, and thus preserve their autonomy while collecting their individual authority into the authority of the state. Unfortunately, our examination of the various arguments in support of majority rule has revealed that this additional claim is unfounded. Whatever else may be said for a majoritarian democracy, it does not appear to be true that the minority remain free and self-ruled while submitting to the majority.

Our failure to discover a form of political association which could combine moral autonomy with legitimate authority is not a result of the imperfect rationality of men, nor of the passions and private interests which deflect men from the pursuit of justice and the general good. Many political philosophers have portrayed the state as a necessary evil forced upon men by their own inability to abide by the principles of morality, or as a tool of one class of men against the others in the never-ending struggle for personal advantage. Marx and Hobbes agree that in a community of men of good will, where the general good guided every citizen, the state would be unnecessary. They differ only in the degree of their hope that so happy a condition can ever be realized.

Nor does our dilemma grow out of the familiar limitations of intellect and knowledge which afflict all but the most extraordinary men. It may be that in a technologically complex world only a few men can hope to master

the major political issues well enough to have genuinely
personal convictions about them. By positing a society of
rational men of good will, however, we have eliminated
such well-known obstacles to the fully just state. The magnitude of our problem is indicated by our inability to solve
the dilemma of autonomy and authority even for a utopian
society! By and large, political philosophers have supposed that utopia was logically possible, however much
they may have doubted that it was even marginally probable. But the arguments of this essay suggest that the just
state must be consigned the category of the round square,
the married bachelor, and the unsensed sense-datum.

If autonomy and authority are genuinely incompatible,
only two courses are open to us. Either we must embrace
philosophical anarchism and treat *all* governments as non-
legitimate bodies whose commands must be judged and
evaluated in each instance before they are obeyed; or else,
we must give up as quixotic the pursuit of autonomy in the
political realm and submit ourselves (by an implicit promise) to whatever form of government appears most just
and beneficent at the moment. (I cannot resist repeating
yet again that if we take this course, *there is no universal
or a priori reason for binding ourselves to a democratic
government rather than to any other sort.* In some situations, it may be wiser to swear allegiance to a benevolent
and efficient dictatorship than to a democracy which im-
poses a tyrannical majority on a defenseless minority. *And
in those cases where we have sworn to obey the rule of the
majority, no additional binding force will exist beyond
what would be present had we promised our allegiance to
a king!*)

It is out of the question to give up the commitment to

moral autonomy. Men are no better than children if they not only accept the rule of others from force of necessity, but embrace it willingly and forfeit their duty unceasingly to weigh the merits of the actions which they perform. When I place myself in the hands of another, and permit him to determine the principles by which I shall guide my behavior, I repudiate the freedom and reason which give me dignity. I am then guilty of what Kant might have called the sin of willful heteronomy.

There would appear to be no alternative but to embrace the doctrine of anarchism and categorically deny *any* claim to legitimate authority by one man over another. Yet I confess myself unhappy with the conclusion that I must simply leave off the search for legitimate collective authority. Perhaps it might be worth saying something about the deeper philosophical reasons for this reluctance.

Man confronts a natural world which is irreducibly *other*, which stands over against him, independent of his will and indifferent to his desires. Only religious superstition or the folly of idealist metaphysics could encourage us to assume that nature will prove ultimately rational, or that the opposition between man and objects must in principle be surmountable. Man also confronts a social world which *appears* other, which *appears* to stand over against him, at least partially independent of his will and frequently capricious in its frustration of his desires. Is it also folly to suppose that this opposition can be overcome, and that man can so perfectly conquer society as to make it his tool rather than his master? To answer this question, we must determine whether the appearance of the objectivity of society is also reality, or whether perhaps here, in the realm of institutions and interpersonal relationships, man's estrangement from the society which dominates him is accidental, adventitious, and ultimately eradicable.

Each individual is born into a social world which is already organized into regular patterns of behavior and expectation. At first, he is aware only of the few persons in his immediate physical environment and of their qualities and appearance. Very soon, the infant learns to expect repeated sequences of behavior from those around him. Later still, the child comes to see these significant persons as playing certain defined roles (mother, father, teacher, policeman) which are also played by other persons in different situations (other children also have mothers and fathers, etc.). The learning of language reinforces this awareness, for built into the word "father" is the notion that there may be many fathers to many children. The child matures and develops a personality by identifying with various role-bearers in his world and internalizing as his own the patterns of behavior and belief which constitute the roles. He *becomes* someone in this way, and also *discovers* who he is by reflecting on the alternatives which life offers him. Characteristically, the adolescent goes through a period of role definition during which he tentatively tries on a variety of roles, in order to test their appropriateness for him. (This is perhaps a description biased by contemporary Western experience. In some cultures, of course, the uncertainty over roles which produces an "identity crisis" never occurs since it is laid down by the society what set of roles the individual shall internalize and act out. For the purposes of this discussion, however, that point is not significant.)

Thus, the social world presents to each individual an objective reality with independently existing structures, just as the physical world does. The infant learns where his body ends and the objects around him begin. He distinguishes between what is within his control (various movements of his body) and what does not respond to his will. In exactly the same way, he learns to recognize the intractable realities of his social environment. When a boy is asked what he wants to be, he is really being asked which already existing social role he wishes to adopt as an adult. His answer—that he wants to be a fireman, or an engineer, or an explorer—indicates that he understands perfectly well the nature of the question. He may see himself, at least in a society like ours, as exercising some control over the roles which he shall adopt; but neither the questioner nor the boy would suppose that either of them has any control over the existence and nature of the roles themselves! Even the social rebel characteristically opts for an existing role, that of bohemian, or beatnik, or revolutionary. Like all role-players, such rebels wear the clothes, live in the quarters, and use the language appropriate to the role which they have chosen.

In any reasonably complex society, social roles are in turn organized into even more extensive patterns of behavior and belief, to which we apply the term "institutions." The church, the state, the army, the market are all such systems of roles. The characteristic interactions of the constituent roles of an institution are determined independently of particular individuals, just as the roles themselves are. At this level of complexity of organization, however, a new phenomenon appears which vastly increases the apparent objectivity of social reality, namely what has come to be known as the "paradox of unintended consequences." Each person in an institutional structure pursues goals and follows patterns at least partially laid down for him by the society—that is, already existing when he takes on the role and hence *given* to him. In his roles, however, he should be able to see the relationship between what he does and what results, even though he may not feel free to alter his goals or try new means. In the process of interaction with other individual role-players, more far-reaching results will be produced which may be neither anticipated nor particularly desired by any person in the system. These unintended consequences will therefore appear to the role-players as somehow not their doing, and hence objective in just the way that natural occurrences are objective. To cite a classic example, as each entrepreneur strives to increase his profit by cutting his price slightly, hoping thereby to seize a larger portion of the total market, the market price of his commodity falls steadily and everyone experiences a decline in profits. If he thinks about it at all, the entrepreneur will characteristically suppose himself to be caught in the grip of a "falling market," which is to say a natural or objective force over which he has no control. Even after he recognizes the causal relationship between his individual act of price-cutting and the drop in the market price, he is liable to think himself powerless to reverse the workings of the "laws of the marketplace." (Perhaps it is worth noting that, contrary to the assumptions of classical liberal economic theory, the entrepreneur is as much in the grip of social forces when he plays the role of capitalist as when he feels the pinch of the market. Even the most casual cross-cultural comparison reveals that "economic man" is a social role peculiar to certain cultures, and not at all the natural man who emerges when the distorting forces of tradition and superstition are lifted.)

The experience of the entrepreneur is reduplicated end-

lessly, so that men come to imagine themselves more completely enslaved by society than they ever were by nature.
Yet their conviction is fundamentally wrong, for while the
natural world really does exist independently of man's
beliefs or desires, and therefore exercises a constraint on
his will which can at best be mitigated or combatted, the
social world is nothing in itself, and consists merely of the
totality of the habits, expectations, beliefs, and behavior
patterns of all the individuals who live in it. To be sure,
insofar as men are ignorant of the total structures of the
institutions within which they play their several roles, they
will be the victims of consequences unintended by anyone;
and, of course, to the extent that men are set against one
another by conflicting interests, those whose institutional
roles give them advantages of power or knowledge in the
social struggle will prevail over those who are relatively
disadvantaged. But since each man's unfreedom is entirely
a result either of ignorance or of a conflict of interests, it
ought to be in principle possible for a society of rational
men of good will to eliminate the domination of society
and subdue it to their wills in a manner that is impossible
in the case of nature.

Consider as an example the economic institutions of
society. At first, men play their several economic roles
(farmer, craftsman, trader, fisherman) in complete ignorance of the network of interactions which influence the
success of their endeavors and guide them into sequences
of decisions, for good or ill, whose structure and ultimate
outcome they cannot see. These same men imagine themselves encapsulated in a set of unchanging economic roles
whose patterns, rewards, and systematic relationships are
quite independent of their wills. Slowly, as the systematic

interconnections themselves become more complex and mutually dependent, man's understanding of the economy as a whole grows, so that, for example, entrepreneurs begin to realize that their profits depend upon the total quantity of goods produced by themselves and their fellow capitalists, and the accumulation of individual desires for those goods which, collectively, constitute the level of demand. The first stage in the mastery of the economy may consist simply in the discovery of such aggregate quantities as demand, supply, interest rate, profit level, and even market price. That is to say, men must *discover* that the interaction of many individual acts of buying and selling establishes a single market price, which reflects the relation of supply to demand of the commodity being marketed. After realizing that such a marketwide price exists, men can begin to understand how it is determined. Only then can they consider the possibility of making that price a direct object of decision, and thus finally free themselves from the tyranny of the market.

In addition to the ignorance which enslaves even those in positions of power in the economy (the capitalists in a laissez-faire system), the pursuit of private interest results in the exploitation and enslavement of those whose roles in the economy carry relatively little power. Hence even the farthest advance imaginable of social knowledge would not suffice to liberate all men from their social bonds unless it were accompanied by a transformation of private interest into a concern for the general good. But if so utopian a condition were achieved, then surely men could once and for all reconquer their common product, society, and at least within the human world, move from the realm of necessity into the realm of freedom. Death and taxes, it is said, are the only certainties in this life; a folk maxim which reflects the deep conviction that men cannot escape the tyranny of either nature or society. Death will always be with us, reminding us that we are creatures of nature. But taxes, along with all the other instruments of social action, are human products, and hence must in the end submit to the collective will of a society of rational men of good will.

It should now be clear why I am unwilling to accept as final the negative results of our search for a political order which harmonizes authority and autonomy. The state is a social institution, and therefore no more than the totality of the beliefs, expectations, habits, and interacting roles of its members and subjects. When rational men, in full knowledge of the proximate and distant consequences of their actions, determine to set private interest aside and pursue the general good, it *must* be possible for them to create a form of association which accomplishes that end without depriving some of them of their moral autonomy. The state, in contrast to nature, cannot be ineradicably *other*.

2. Utopian Glimpses of a World Without States

Through the exercise of *de facto* legitimate authority, states achieve what Max Weber calls the imperative coordination of masses of men and women. To some extent, of course, this coordination consists in the more-or-less voluntary submission by large numbers of people to institutional arrangements which are directly contrary to their interests. Threats of violence or economic sanction play a central role in holding the people in line, although as Weber very persuasively argues, the myth of legitimacy is also an important instrument of domination.

But even if there were no exploitation or domination in society, it would still be in men's interest to achieve a very high level of social coordination, for reasons both of economic efficiency and of public order. At our present extremely advanced stage of division of labor, relatively minor disruptions of social coordination can produce a breakdown of the flow of goods and services necessary to sustain life.

Consequently, it is worth asking whether a society of men who have been persuaded of the truth of anarchism—a society in which no one claims legitimate authority or would believe such a claim if it were made—could through alternative methods achieve an adequate level of social coordination.

There are, so far as I can see, three general sorts of purposes, other than the domination and exploitation of one segment of society by another, for which men might wish to achieve a high order of social coordination. First, there is the collective pursuit of some *external* national goal such as national defense, territorial expansion, or economic imperialism. Second, there is the collective pursuit of some *internal* goal which requires the organization and coordination of the activities of large numbers of people, such as traffic safety, to cite a trivial example, or the reconstruction of our cities, to cite an example not so trivial. Finally, there is the maintenance of our industrial economy whose functional differentiation and integration—to use the sociologist's jargon—are advanced enough to sustain an adequately high level of production. Is there any way in which these ends could be served other than by commands enforced by coercion and by the myth of legitimacy?

I do not now have a complete and coherent answer to this question, which is in a way the truest test of the political philosophy of anarchism, but I shall make a few suggestions which may open up fruitful avenues of investigation.

With regard to matters of national defense and foreign adventure, it seems to me that there is much to be said for the adoption of a system of voluntary compliance with governmental directives. If we assume a society of anarchists— a society, that is to say, which has achieved a level of moral and intellectual development at which superstitious beliefs in legitimacy of authority have evaporated—then the citizenry would be perfectly capable of choosing freely whether to defend the nation and carry its purpose beyond the national borders. The army itself could be run on the basis of voluntary commitments and submission to orders. To be sure, the day might arrive when there were not enough volunteers to protect the freedom and security of the society. But if that were the case, then it would clearly be illegitimate to command the citizens to fight. Why should a nation continue to exist if its populace does not wish to defend it? One thinks here of the contrast between the Yugoslav partisans or Israeli soldiers, on the one hand, and the American forces in Vietnam on the other.

The idea of voluntary compliance with governmental directives is hardly new, but it inevitably provokes the shocked reaction that social chaos would result from any such procedure. My own opinion is that superstition rather than reason lies behind this reaction. I personally would feel quite safe in an America whose soldiers were free to choose when and for what they would fight.

Voluntary compliance would go far toward generating sufficient social coordination to permit collective pursuit of domestic goals as well. In addition, I believe that much could be done through the local, community-based development of a consensual or general will with regard to matters of collective rather than particular interest. In the concluding chapter of my book, *The Poverty of Liberalism*, I have offered a conceptual analysis of the several modes of community. I will simply add that achievement of the sorts of community I analyzed there would require a far-reaching decentralization of the American economy.

This last point brings me to the most difficult problem of all—namely, the maintenance of a level of social coordination sufficient for an advanced industrial economy. As Friedrich Hayek and a number of other classical liberal political economists have pointed out, the natural operation of the market is an extremely efficient way of coordinating human behavior on a large scale without coercion or appeal to authority. Nevertheless, reliance on the market is fundamentally irrational once men know how to control it in order to avoid its undesired consequences. The original laissez-faire liberals viewed the laws of the market as objective laws of a benevolent nature; modern laissez-faire liberals propose that we go on confusing nature and society, even though we have the knowledge to subordinate the market to our collective will and decision.

Only extreme economic decentralization could permit the sort of voluntary economic coordination consistent with the ideals of anarchism and affluence. At the present time, of course, such decentralization would produce economic chaos, but if we possessed a cheap, local source of power and an advanced technology of small-scale production, and if we were in addition willing to accept a high level of economic waste, we might be able to break the American economy down into regional and subregional units of manageable size. The exchanges between the units would be inefficient and costly—very large inventory levels, inelasticities of supply and demand, considerable waste, and so forth. But in return for this price, men would have increasing freedom to act autonomously. In effect, such a society would enable all men to be autonomous agents, whereas in our present society, the relatively few autonomous men are—as it were—parasitic upon the obedient, authority-respecting masses.

These remarks fall far short of a coherent projection of an anarchist society, but they may serve to make the ideal seem a bit less like a mere fantasy of utopian political philosophy.

Index